POETS *talk*

POETS *talk*

Pauline Butling and Susan Rudy

Conversations with

Robert Kroetsch,

Daphne Marlatt,

Erin Mouré,

Dionne Brand,

Marie Annharte Baker,

Jeff Derksen *and*

Fred Wah

The University of Alberta Press

Published by

The University of Alberta Press
Ring House 2
Edmonton, Alberta, Canada T6G 2E1

Copyright © Pauline Butling and Susan Rudy 2005

ISBN 0–88864–431–0

Library and Archives Canada Cataloguing in Publication Data

Butling, Pauline
    Poets talk : conversations with Robert Kroetsch, Daphne Marlatt, Erin Mouré,
Dionne Brand, Marie Annharte Baker, Jeff Derksen and Fred Wah /
Pauline Butling and Susan Rudy.

Includes bibliographical references and index.
ISBN 0–88864–431–0

    1. Poetics. 2. Creation (Literary, artistic, etc.) 3. Poets, Canadian
(English)—20th century—Interviews. I. Rudy, Susan, 1961– II. Title.

PS8155.1.B88 2004   808.1   C2004–907160–2

Printed and bound in Canada.
First edition, first printing, 2005

All rights reserved.

A volume in (*cuRRents*), a Canadian literature series. Jonathan Hart, series editor.

The University of Alberta Press is committed to protecting our natural environment. As part
of our efforts, this book is printed on stock produced by New Leaf Paper: it contains 100%
post-consumer recycled fibres and is acid- and chlorine-free.

The University of Alberta Press gratefully acknowledges the support received for its
publishing program from The Canada Council for the Arts. The University of Alberta
Press also gratefully acknowledges the financial support of the Government of Canada
through the Book Publishing Industry Development Program (BPDIP) and from the Alberta
Foundation for the Arts for our publishing activities.

CONTENTS

Preface vii
Acknowledgements ix
Introduction xi

one "Historicizing Postmodernism" with Robert Kroetsch 1
    Pauline Butling & Susan Rudy

two On Salvaging: A Conversation with Daphne Marlatt 23
    Pauline Butling & Susan Rudy

three "Why not be excessive?": A Conversation with Erin Mouré 43
    Pauline Butling & Susan Rudy

four Dionne Brand on Struggle and Community, Possibility
    and Poetry 63
    Pauline Butling

five "I make sense of my world through writing"
    An Interview with Marie Annharte Baker 89
    Pauline Butling

six A Conversation on "Cultural Poetics" with Jeff Derksen 115
    Pauline Butling & Susan Rudy

seven Fred Wah on Hybridity and Asianicity in Canada 143
    Susan Rudy

Works Cited 171
Index 187

Preface

POETS TALK: *Conversations with Robert Kroetsch, Daphne Marlatt, Erin Mouré, Dionne Brand, Marie Annharte Baker, Jeff Derksen and Fred Wah* developed out of a research project on innovative poetry in English Canada that we began in 1991. We had met in Calgary two years previously—when we both moved there—and had quickly formed a friendship based on shared interests, including an interest in contemporary writing. We often found ourselves puzzling over a new book, or talking about a recent poetry reading, or sharing ideas about how to teach contemporary writing. Calgary, like most Canadian cities, has a steady stream of visiting writers in any given year. In Calgary there is a high percentage of readings by experimental poets, both because of the focus on innovative poetics in the Creative Writing Program at the University of Calgary following Fred Wah's appointment to the English/Creative Writing faculty in 1989, and because of the seemingly boundless energy of Calgary's young poets in the 1990s who sponsored readings, started magazines, and sparked debates and arguments everywhere. They include Ashok Mathur, Nicole Markotic, derek beaulieu, Jacqueline Turner, Suzette Mayr, Hiromi Goto, Rita Wong, Jeff Derksen, tom muir, and Jill Hartman—poets who were associated with *absinthe, filling Station*, the Calgary Women of Colour Collective, *endnote, Dandelion / dANDelion*, and other oppositional sites.

In our discussions, we often groped for a language. Feminism had given us critical methods for understanding gendered reading and writing practices. But now there were new questions—about identity formation, cultural appropriation, and forms of oppression based on race, class, and sexuality. Who speaks for whom? What is the poet's relation to community? How do new subjects gain visibility? How do race, class, and sexuality impact poetic practice? The most useful tools and terms that we could find came from the poets, not only in their poetry but also in the essays, reviews, talks, interviews and other prose works that they wrote as they engaged with the complexities of 1990s identity politics and related social/poetic issues. Let us go talk to the poets we said.

Over many glasses of wine or cups of coffee, we did more than a dozen interviews in Calgary throughout the 1990s, all of them accompanied by much laughter and general revelry. Rambling informal conversations were the norm, which meant considerable editing and follow-up email discussions to clarify or extend points. At first we saw the interviews as companions to the critical essays that we were writing on Marlatt, Wah, Mouré, Derksen, and Kroetsch. Then we decided to do the opposite—hence the interviews with Brand, Baker (and several others not included here*). Then the project became too large for one book. The essays became *Writing in Our Time: Canada's Radical Poetries in English 1957–2003* (Wilfrid Laurier University Press 2005) and the interviews became *Poets Talk*.

The interviews more than fulfilled their purpose in providing a language for talking about some of the innovative writing of the decade. Taken together, they offer a forum on poetics, a dialogue on the *what* and *why* of poetry during a decade of seismic shifts in poetic thought and practice. This publication exists only because we were able to take part in that dialogue. We thank the poets for their generosity in making time to talk with us, and for their patience in working through the editing process.

—*Pauline Butling & Susan Rudy*

* They include Ayanna Black, Di Brandt, Victor Coleman, Steve McCaffery, Roy Miki, Lola Tostevin, and the Kootenay School of Writing Collective of 1992. Audio tape recordings of the interviews are archived at the Special Collections, MacKimmie Library, University of Calgary, except for two (Tostevin and McCaffery) that mysteriously turned out to be blank.

Acknowledgements

WE COULD NOT HAVE COMPLETED THIS PROJECT WITHOUT THE intellectual engagement and emotional support provided by our extended families of spouses, daughters, friends, colleagues, students, and writers here in Calgary and elsewhere. Several undergraduate and graduate students acted as transcribers and research assistants, including Susan Holbrook, Cindy McMann, Stephen Morton, Karen McLaughlin, Megan Roach, Jason Wiens, and B.J. Wray. We thank them for their diligence and enthusiasm.

Finally, we gratefully acknowledge the generous support of the Social Sciences and Humanities Research Council of Canada, the Killam Foundation, the Centre for Women's Studies and Gender Relations at the University of British Columbia, the Centre for Research and Teaching on Women at McGill University, as well as our own institutions, the University of Calgary and the Alberta College of Art & Design.

Introduction

The Poets

YOU ARE ABOUT TO LISTEN IN ON CONVERSATIONS WITH SEVEN OF
the most innovative and socially conscious poets writing today.
Robert Kroetsch, Daphne Marlatt, Erin Mouré, Dionne Brand,
Marie Annharte Baker, Jeff Derksen and Fred Wah are poets who, as
Dionne Brand puts it, "take up the hard questions":

> I count myself in that tradition of writers who take up the
> hard questions, who are never satisfied with our condition,
> who want to see equality in the world and who will push
> their ideas and their language and their minds to embrace
> that.... I count myself lucky to be part of that genealogy....
> Much as it is sometimes denounced, it is still the most
> important poetry that has been written.
>
> (Interview with da Costa).

This poetry is important because it unsettles habits of thought and
perception, because it pushes language, because it offers points of
ignition and resistance within and against the social order. Louis
Cabri calls it the "social lyric": "some poets...accept the...historical
fact of social encodings in order to further both a fundamental
critique of, and a change upon," those encodings.* In our discussions

---

* Cabri differentiates the poet of the "social lyric" from the individualist, who
"reject[s] 'society' outright, often in order to critique it from an elsewhere
that is traditionally figured as 'nature.'"

in *Poets Talk*, questions about innovative forms and processes are linked to "hard questions" about citizenship, relationships, subjectivity, language, and power. We ask, what is at stake in their formal experimentation? Why do they reinvent poetic forms? Why use unconventional punctuation, interrupted syntax, repetition, fragmentation, and disjunction? What is the poet's role in the poem? How is oppositional poetics linked to social critique? You will not find easy answers here, but there are some common threads. They all emphasize the production of meaning over its consumption, they treat the poem as a construction—or reconstruction—rather than a vehicle for self-expression, and their discussions of form invariably extend into questions about the relation of language and form to hegemonic systems.

Unlike *the* Group of Seven, however, these seven poets did not begin with a shared polemic. Indeed they speak from different regions, generations, sexualities, classes, races, and communities and their lives have followed very different trajectories. Fred Wah and Daphne Marlatt were associated with Vancouver's TISH (1961–63 for Wah, 1963–64 for Marlatt) at the start of their writing careers. They share an interest in the localism of William Carlos Williams and Charles Olson and in the oppositional politics and poetics of the Black Mountain and Beat poets. Robert Kroetsch also discovered Williams and Olson among others in the 1960s but he did so from a different location, as part of the matrix that produced *boundary 2, an international journal of postmodern literature* at the State University of New York in Binghamton. Dionne Brand and Marie Annharte Baker both began writing the 1970s: Brand was inspired by the Black Power and Pan-African movements and the work of young Black writers, such as Nikki Giovanni, Amiri Baraka, and Sonia Sanchez; Annharte by her work with the Indian Youth Council, Alliance for Red Power, and by the example of free-thinking women writers of the 1940s and 1950s in Paris and New York. Jeff Derksen and Erin Mouré share, as points of origin, the class-conscious poetics that developed in opposition to the right wing politics of the 1980s but Mouré's connections were to the Vancouver Industrial Writers Union, Derksen's to the Kootenay School of Writing. In the 1980s and 1990s they all shifted ground in response to various personal and social imperatives: Mouré, Marlatt and Brand explored feminist, lesbian politics and poetics; Wah and Annharte articulated a racialized subjectivity; Derksen and Mouré increasingly engaged with the 1990s discourses of civic responsibility; and Robert Kroetsch extended the critique of gender roles that he began in the 1970s and 1980s. Yet, despite their divergent tracks, they often show up together at conferences, in magazines, anthologies, and other sites that focus on innovative thought and practice because, as Brand says, they are part of a genealogy of poets who "push their ideas and their language and their minds."

The Interviews

We begin with Robert Kroetsch, who takes us back to a formative moment in the 1960s, when he ran across Roland Barthes' *Writing Degree Zero* in a London (England) bookstore, sparking a life-long interest in poststructuralist theory. That interest expanded, he explains, when he took a job at the State University of New York in Binghamton, met William Spanos, and with Spanos, founded one of the most innovative literary journals of the 1960s and 1970s, *boundary 2, an international journal of postmodern literature.* Kroetsch's oppositional poetics, however, stems as much from his perceived outsider position as a rural Albertan and young male who did not fit the Western, macho prototype. He speaks at length about his poetics—his mistrust of line endings, the subversive value of sub-literary forms, his dread of systems, and his need to "destroy" grammar to disturb settled meanings. We discuss "Poem for My Dead Sister" (*A Likely Story*) and *Revisions of Letters Already Sent* in detail.

Our conversation with Daphne Marlatt focuses on the connections between Marlatt's feminist politics and her subversive writing practices. She explains that she undermines literary forms and grammatical conventions because they do not fit her experience as a woman and, later on, as a lesbian. For Marlatt, the poem is a "neural network" where sparks fly, tensions build, words collide and regroup. As such, it is a place to generate semantic slippages and alternative pathways. Much of the interview focuses on Marlatt's *Salvage*, both in terms of her intention "to write in lesbian" and her innovative use of the prose poem. Her "salvage" work, she explains, which involves rewriting poems from as far back as twenty years, is informed by a lesbian consciousness, but is not simply a rewriting. It's "like painting over an old canvas where you're painting over figures that are already there and at the same time you're uncovering some of them." She turned to the prose poem because she "came to feel very restricted in verse form." In *Steveston* and again in *Salvage*, she developed the "stanzagraph" as a compositional unit, its shape determined by the flow of language and thought down the page. We discuss "Booking Passage" (*Salvage* 115–19) in detail.

Erin Mouré locates her work within community contexts, noting the crucial role of the Montreal community of feminist writer/theorists that she met when she moved to Montreal in the 1980s to her formation as a poet. Also important to her formation was her work with the Vancouver Industrial Writers Union of the late 1970s and early 1980s (Phil Hall, Tom Wayman and others) where she first began to think about class. More recently, theories of perception, brain function, and citizenship have been central to her poetry. She notes parallels between the "synaptic experience" described by brain theorists, which is the process of "jumping to something new," and the "jumps" in the poems in *Sheepish Beauty, Civilian Love*. In her words: "If you're writing poetry, you can't go one way all the time. You have to get off the track. You have jumps to make. Or you keep writing the same old poem, the 'cultural poem.'" She also discusses her long-standing interest in civic responsibility and how that impacts an individual life and practice, especially for a lesbian writer, who is often excluded from the civic. Two poems are discussed in detail, "blue spruce" and "the Notification of Birches" from *Sheepish Beauty, Civilian Love*.

Dionne Brand also notes that her formation as a poet relates to her experience of outsider positions, in her case, a race-identified position. Growing up in the colonized world of Jamaica, she explains, she only gradually discovered some of the resistant literary and political texts that provided alternatives to what she calls "the slavishness...of a Naipaul for British culture." Her politicization continued, following her move to Toronto in 1970, when she discovered American Black activist writers such as Sonia Sanchez, Nikki Giovanni, Gwendolyn Brooks, and Amiri Baraka. Thus began her life-long involvement in left politics and community work. She talks about her sojourn in Grenada in 1979 on the heels of their revolution, which coincided with her coming out as a lesbian. In terms of her writing practices, she discusses her resistance to the colonizing effects of "standard English," as in her use of the demotic as a rhythmic structure in "No Language is Neutral." Brand also describes her work in oral history, film, and fiction as part of her literary activism, while recognizing that if she wants her "life represented in its fullness and its beauty then it takes the form of poetry."

Annharte tells a story of a similarly strong link between her poetics and politics. She recalls that one of her first pieces of writing was titled "Manifesto for First People" and characterizes herself as a "word warrior" who fights racism by taking on the racist slurs and bureaucratic terms that diminish Native people. Annharte's work in poetry was hampered for many years, she explains, because a high school experience of date rape resulted in self-silencing. In the process of writing *Being on the Moon*, which was written over a twelve-year period, poetry became a "safe place" where she could create her own medicine, "the poem became a personal friend/advisor." She credits bpNichol with prompting her to think in terms of a book when she took his summer writing workshop at Red Deer in 1988. Annharte also explains that she favours humour rather than anger as her mode of expression and discusses her use of jokes, street language, satire, anecdotes, and other comic devices in *Coyote Columbus Cafe*. Her goal is to de-program the demeaning voice within Native people as much as to critique pervasive societal racism. She also likes disjunctive techniques, such as the ellipses dots in "Dark Love" (*Being on the Moon* 35) that represent a "tuning in and out of consciousness"; and the process of "sketching," which creates a rush or flood of detail that builds momentum and then "falls off the cliff" at the end of the line, as in "Raced Out to Write this Up" (*Being on the Moon* 60). The interview concludes with a discussion of several poems from *Exercises in Lip Pointing*.

In the interview with Jeff Derksen, we focus on what Derksen calls "cultural poetics," by which he means a poetics that works within the structures of power to disarticulate and rearticulate the "linkages within the system," rather than a poetics that posits a detached position. The first step toward re-articulation is to perform/reveal the contradictions *within* social systems, he explains, even as he recognizes that he is determined by those conditions. In *Down Time*, Derksen writes from a subject position that is determined by working class conditions. In *Dwell*, he performs "the tensions between nationalism and regionalism." In "All Mod Contradictions" [*Transnational Muscle Cars*], he engages the tensions within global capitalism. Derksen's story of his formation as a poet begins with serendipitous encounters such as taking a first-year poetry course from George Bowering at Simon Fraser University in 1976, discovering Canadian writing in the New Westminster public library, or going to David Thompson University Centre (DTUC) after a chance encounter with Tom Wayman who was on a recruiting trip in the Vancouver area. At DTUC, he explains, he not only took a degree in Creative Writing and English, working with Fred Wah, Tom Wayman, Colin Browne and others; he also began to combine political activism and poetry by taking part in the protests over the British Columbia government closure of DTUC in 1984. His politicized poetics developed further as a member of The Kootenay School of Writing (KSW) collective in Vancouver where he worked with Tom Wayman, Deanna Ferguson, Nancy Shaw, Dorothy Trujillo Lusk, Kevin Davies and others to set up an alternative "school" of workshops and readings. He also notes the importance of the American Language writers to his "cultural poetics," especially following the New Poetics Colloquium held in Vancouver in 1985 together with the KSW workshops that he attended in the late 1980s with Susan Howe, Charles Bernstein, Lyn Hejinian, Bruce Andrews, and Abigail Child. In terms of poetic practice, Derksen characterizes his work as "hyperreferential" or flooded with meaning, rather than non-referential. He discusses "Neighbourhood" and "Excursives 1.2.3" (*Dwell*) in terms of some of specific applications of his "cultural poetics."

The interview with Fred Wah begins with questions about Wah's increasing engagement with race and identity politics in the 1980s and 1990s. Wah explains that a "dialogue about Asianicity" was not available to him until the late 1970s. It developed from the documentary poems of the 1970s that explored ethnicity, such as Daphne Marlatt's *Steveston* and Andrew Suknaski's *Wood Mountain Poems*, and from activities such as the Japanese Canadian Redress movement. Wah's own poetry, he explains, became inflected by race when he began writing about his father in *Breathin' My Name with a Sigh* and *Waiting for Saskatchewan*. In terms of specific writing strategies, Wah explains that his discovery of a reflexive "you" enabled him to engage his mixed race identity because he could play with interpellating the self in the poem. Wah also links his use of hybrid forms, such as the utaniki (*Grasp the Sparrow's Tale*), the haibun ("Father/Mother Haibun"), the prose poem (*Breathin' My Name with a Sigh*), and the biotext (*Diamond Grill*) to his exploration of racial hybridity. "Father/Mother Haibun #7" (*Waiting for Saskatchewan*) is discussed in detail in terms of both poetic experiments and the father/mother content. In general, Wah, using terms suggested by Miriam Nichols, characterizes his poetics as a "poetics of process as opposed to the poetics of knowledge" (Nichols 116–17); knowledge unfolds in the process of writing. The interview ends with Wah confirming his commitment to the "social lyric." In his words: "I believe that writing is only interesting if it offers possibilities for shifts in consciousness, and hopefully shifts in the way we experience the world."

Why Bother?

There can be no mistaking the commitment to social change for all the above poets: they critique "social encodings" (Cabri above), they push for "shifts in consciousness…shifts in the way we experience the world" (Wah above), and, paradoxically, as they push against the social, they embrace it. That seriousness of purpose alone might be sufficient reason to value their writing and to invest time in reading it. It was certainly one reason why we started this project. However the answer to "why bother" is also more mundane, simply that it was so much fun to sit down and talk with these writers for a while. We offer *Poets Talk* as much to share that pleasure. Poets who "take up the hard questions," who "push their ideas and their language and their minds" (Brand above) are endlessly curious, lively, mischievous, funny, and provocative. You will surely enjoy spending a couple of hours in their company.

—*Pauline Butling & Susan Rudy*

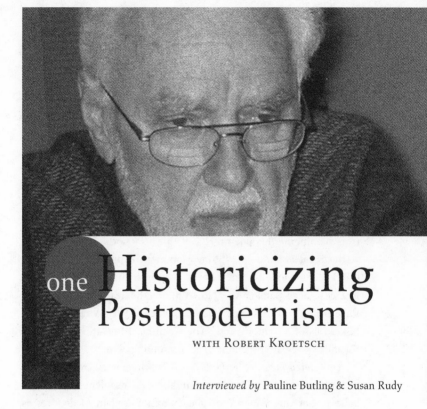

one Historicizing Postmodernism

WITH ROBERT KROETSCH

Interviewed by Pauline Butling & Susan Rudy

WINNIPEG-BASED POET, NOVELIST, CRITIC, AND TEACHER Robert Kroetsch was born in a homestead shack in 1927 in Heisler, Alberta. After earning an undergraduate degree in literature and philosophy from the University of Alberta in 1948, he worked for six years in the Canadian North—on riverboats on the Mackenzie River, and for the United States Air Force in Goose Bay, Labrador— before earning graduate degrees from Middlebury College, Vermont (M.A. 1956) and the Writers Workshop at the University of Iowa (Ph.D. 1961). An English professor at the State University of New York at Binghamton from 1961–78, he and colleague William Spanos founded the journal of postmodern writing *boundary 2, an international journal of postmodern literature.* Kroetsch was general editor of *boundary 2*'s "A Canadian Issue" (1974). In 1978 he returned to Canada to teach writing and literature, for one year at the University of Calgary and for many years at the University of Manitoba, where he is now Professor Emeritus. He has been a mentor and much loved friend to hundreds of students, many of whom have themselves become distinguished writers.

Kroetsch is internationally known as a poet and novelist and widely acknowledged in Canada for his challenges to the conventions of literary criticism and theory, claiming that "criticism is really a version of story" (Neuman and Wilson *Labyrinths* 30). Since at least the early 1960s he has worked "ceaselessly to extend the limits of Canadian fiction and poetry" (Spanos 120). Poems written and published in little magazines (including *Alphabet, The Canadian Forum, Fiddlehead,* and *Grain*) from 1960–75 appear in *The Stone Hammer Poems* (1975), a collection that remains formally original, gently comic, and acutely intelligent: "This paperweight on my desk // where I begin / this poem was // found in a wheatfield / lost (this hammer, / this poem). // Cut to a function, / this stone was / (the hand is gone—" ("Stone Hammer Poem" 54). *Field Notes* (1981) uses "Stone Hammer Poem" as a prologue, followed by "The Ledger," "Seed Catalogue," "How I Joined the Seal Herd," "The Sad Phoenician," "The Silent Poet Sequence, "The Winnipeg Zoo," "Sketches of a Lemon" and "The Criminal Intensities of Love as Paradise"—the first sections of a continuing poem.

Completed Field Notes (1989) collects the poetry from 1973–88 when Kroetsch claims to have come to "a poet's silence": "I like to believe that the sequence of poems, announced in medias res as continuing, is, in its acceptance of its own impossibilities, completed" (*Completed Field Notes* 269). Throughout the 1990s he continued to publish suspiciously poetic-looking texts under the title "The Poetics of Rita Kleinhart" in little magazines (including *Open Letter, West Coast Line, Prairie Fire*), many of which appear in *The Hornbooks of Rita K* (2001), nominated for the Governor General's Award for Poetry. These "hornbooks," ostensibly written by Kroetsch's alter-ego, a prairie woman writer named Rita Kleinhart, are introduced to readers through the voice of her lover and editor, Raymond, who simultaneously addresses her: "Rita, you are wont to write a crabbed and stubborn / sentence, but this beats all. Without so much as a word / you point straight through the dark and past the bend in / the highway to the sign on the restaurant roof that, / glowingly, says // EATS" (104). A second edition of the *Completed Field Notes* appeared in 2000 with an introduction by Fred Wah. Kroetsch was honoured with the Manitoba Arts Council Award of Distinction in 2004. In Kroetsch's latest book, *The Snowbird Poems* (2004), the main character, travelling with the mysterious Henrietta, heads south for the winter and reflects on life: "We fly south to forget winter and instead / we remember the long color of snow" (57).

Kroetsch's poetry has been anthologized extensively. See *The New Long Poem Anthology* (ed. Thesen 1991, 2001), *Uncommon Wealth: An Anthology of Poetry in English* (ed. Besner et al. 1997), *15 Canadian Poets x 3* (ed. Geddes 4th edition 2001), and *A New Anthology of Canadian Literature in English* (eds. Bennett and Brown 2002). For further information about Kroetsch's decades of work as a novelist and critic see Brian Edward's entry on Kroetsch in the *Routledge Encyclopedia of Post-Colonial Literatures in English* (1994). Recent critical work includes Nanjo, "Canadian Absences and American Presences in the Poetry of Robert Kroetsch" (2002), Yougmin, "The Experimental Spirit in Canadian Poetry" (2003), and Bertacco, *Out of Place: The Writings of Robert Kroetsch* (2002). See also Spanos, "Retrieving Bob Kroetsch on the Occasion of His Seventieth Birthday" (1999) and Sellery, "Robert Kroetsch and Aritha van Herk on Writing & Reading Gender and Genres: An Interview" (2001).

—SR

one

Susan Rudy: In "A Canadian Issue" of *boundary* 2 (1974) you infamously wrote: "Canadian literature evolved directly from Victorian into Postmodern" (1).* We understand your use of the term "postmodern" to signify writing since the 1960s that, in Canada at least, is conscious of its materiality and historicity.

Pauline Butling: So could you talk about your own historical contexts, the particular books, for instance, that made it possible for you to write how and what you were writing in the 1960s, 1970s, and 1980s?

Robert Kroetsch: Actually, in 1963 I was in England on a vacation. In London I happened onto two books. One of them was Roland Barthes' *Writing Degree Zero*, that wee little first edition that

---

* The full context of Kroetsch's cryptic statement is worth quoting: "Canadian literature evolved directly from Victorian into Postmodern. Morley Callaghan went to Paris and met the Modern writers; he, for Canada, experienced the real and symbolic encounter; he, heroically and successfully, resisted. The country that invented Marshall McLuhan and Northrop Frye did so by not ever being Modern" ("A Canadian Issue" 1).

came out, and the other was the stories of Jorge Luis Borges in English, so both were in translation. It was just amazing to hear there were new ways of thinking about language, narrative, meaning. And I began reading a bit, but in total isolation until we hired Bill [William] Spanos at the State University of New York [at Binghamton] around 1968.

Susan: So you went from England to go back to Binghamton?

Robert: Well, I was just on summer vacation in England. I was already teaching in Binghamton where I had been instrumental in hiring Bill. A lot of people had never heard of the things he was talking about, but I had, so we hired him. He and I became quite good friends and he said "let's start this journal," and I said "there's no use starting a journal unless there's something new to be said, because there are a lot of journals in the United States." But he thought that there should be a place to discuss what he called "this whole thing that comes after Modernism."

Pauline: Where did you get the term postmodernism?

Robert: Oh that's the irony, we said, "well, how can we identify our journal as being about this?" We tried a lot of things, I don't remember what they were, and Bill said, "well what about *boundary 2*?" Because the first *boundary* was Modernist—very Poundian—and this journal would be moving out of Modernism, so it's a second *boundary*. And he liked the pun. Then we thought, well that's such a mysterious title we better have a subtitle—at first I think it was *a journal of postmodern literature*. We had seen the word "postmodernism" used a couple of times. I have no idea where we got the term but we said, "well, it sounds like kind of a neutral word." Little did we know we had brought the avengers upon our heads, but we decided to call it *a journal of postmodern writing*.

Pauline: Were you aware of the theory of so-called postmodernism then or were you aware of a number of writers that you wanted to publish that you thought were doing something different?

Robert: We knew there was an emerging theory, but it was very muddy. Spanos at that time was very Heideggerian. In fact, Spanos was really more into philosophy than literature in many ways, and he used to be astonished when I would read a text closely. He hadn't thought of doing that. So we worked together. Well, I knew very little theory then. Before Bill got there I had taught my first graduate course; I got a notice in the mail one day saying "you're going to teach summer school"—and I said I had planned to go away. Well, change your plans, buddy, they said. And I was told that as recompense I would teach a graduate course, so I taught American Literature. And again, you study things, but when you start teaching them, you read them in a different way. [William Carlos] Williams and [Wallace] Stevens were the beginning—and I saw that nobody was talking about the poems the way I was reading them. I mean this notion of "gap" and what we now would call deconstruction. Even a poem like "The Snow," or is it "The Snowman," by Stevens, where you have to be cold for a long time before you realize the tree isn't cold. We started getting into accidents—I went to the West Coast to give a reading…

Pauline: The U.S. West Coast?

Robert: Yes, and I came back, and I said, "you know, people are talking about Jack Spicer a lot out there." And Bill said, "well, let's find out why." Spicer was not known in the East at all, and so we did an issue on Jack Spicer.

Pauline: You had no contact with the State University of New York at Buffalo?

Robert: Very little.

Pauline: Were you aware of anything going on in Canada in the 1960s?

Robert: Well, I was aware of bpNichol and I had been reading the TISH people very early on. In 1965 when my first novel came out I went on tour across Canada, and I started meeting writers. And I knew of Warren Tallman. But "A Canadian Issue" of *boundary* 2 really clarified for me where I stood, whose side of the fence I was on.

Pauline: Did the presence of these writers give you permission to write in different ways, or did it give you models? Or were those things that you were cooking up yourself? Did you find things elsewhere that were useful to you?

Robert: In teaching I used [Charles] Olson a lot. Even in trying to deal with that fanaticism, I learned things. And then of course, New York City kids were aware of [John] Ashbery as a real regional hero there, so many of their poems sounded like Ashbery. It was quite amazing. And Ashbery's openness about kinds of discourse and his notion of the pronoun hanging loose were useful.

Pauline: This is jumping ahead a bit, but through most of *Field Notes,* I see connections to Olson, the way you mix up all those different voices in the poem and the way you use margins.

Robert: Yes, when I taught my first graduate course in 1964 I listed on the syllabus the long poems of Wallace Stevens. And a senior professor came and said, "I hope you know that nobody can make sense of those poems." An older professor was going to save me from myself. And so then of course [Olson's] *The Maximus Poems* were just natural for me. Even then, I had this obsession about place, I didn't know why, and how to write place. And I guess if there was a moment of illumination, it was when I read those three words in Williams: "a local pride." That named what I, in my bones, was trying to do.

Pauline: But your model is very different from Olson's and Williams' because Olson lived in Gloucester and Williams lived in Paterson, but you have not lived in one place.

Robert: Well, that's one reason why somebody like [Daphne] Marlatt interested me. That in a Canadian poem, you didn't live there. I mean she was marginally there but...

Pauline: Do you mean *Vancouver Poems,* or *Steveston?*

Robert: I was thinking of *Steveston.*

Susan: Are you also talking about the fact that she wasn't born in Canada?

Robert: No, I meant that in *Paterson,* a man was living in or very near Paterson and for us it had sort of slipped away, that town.

Pauline: Well I wonder if it has something to do with the fact that Canadians are almost embarrassed about place, or place of origin, because it isn't valued. Fred [Wah] wrote his *Mountain* and *Lardeau* from Buffalo, for example, whereas for Williams it was possible to write from your own place.

Robert: That notion that if your place was ugly or whatever you still had to see it through somehow was incredibly important for me. In fact, my area [in Heisler, Alberta] now looks more beautiful to me than it did then, but that's because my sense of beauty has changed, I guess.

Susan: Isn't it having the freedom to have left, and then look back?

Robert: Oh, I think so, and that also raises serious questions for me.

Pauline: About nostalgia?

Susan: And who can leave and why?

Robert: Or where it's located in time, the place, you know, that's kind of fixing it. Like the Heisler we went to see this week is really very different from the one of my childhood.

Pauline: I'll bet you never thought of it as a beautiful farm.

Robert: No, I just wanted to get the hell out of there.

Pauline: To get back to the sixties, when were you in Binghamton?

Robert: I was there from 1961 to 1978. And you see, even on our campus we had a war going on, which made me think more clearly, I guess, about these things. But Bill and I were from whatever you want to call that school—Olson, Pound, and so on. He and his students were often very vehement about Olson's poetics. I wanted to make up a list of visitors, about who'd be allowed on campus! So it was fun in that sense; you really had to take a stand.

Pauline: That's my sense of the sixties too, that it was really a contested space.

Robert: And a real political system was behind it. So much was at stake. People wouldn't come to readings we organized, for instance. It was not a matter of listening, it was a matter of making a statement by not listening. Another person who was very important at that time was [Robert] Creeley.

Pauline: Did you make contact with Creeley when he went to the State University of New York at Buffalo in 1965?

Robert: Yes, we had a lot of fun; he and Spanos had a long correspondence. So Creeley was very important to us even though I personally didn't pick up on Creeley's poetics at all. I was much more interested in *The Maximus Poems.* The looser they got, as he was losing control of it, the better I liked them.

Pauline: Creeley works very much with the line, and that's another question I wanted to ask you. You say somewhere that you don't care very much about the line.

Robert: Yes, I said that when I realized the crisis is located in the line.

Pauline: But I'm curious about how you work with the line. You don't torque the line like Creeley does, for example.

Robert: Oh I don't, no, not at all. I think my greatest anxiety is about the end, line-ending. We grew up, my generation, grew up believing that all the action came at the end of the line. Whether it was rhyme or off rhyme or whatever. And I resented that. Put the action somewhere else, you know? I'm not so sure I've ever figured it out. Maybe my virtue is in not having figured it out. But later today [at a reading in Calgary] I'm going to read from a poem I'm writing, "Revisions of Letters Already Sent" where there are passages like "delete the following:" "insert the following." There is a letter we've all written and sent, so to speak, in the world, and you want to rewrite it somehow or other, or correct it, or revise it. It's like "always already" there or whatever. The Heideggerian thing? And I feel I could go on for a long time exploring this. Sometimes I might just send "delete this word." There's one incident I use about seeing a butterfly. But the fragment as I use it comes out as lines somehow. They aren't simply prose pieces. The notion of line often asserts itself.

Please insert where indicated

the butterfly by the water tank, that morning of my childhood, was large beyond any butterfly I had ever dared to imagine, a brighter yellow (or was it orange?), patterned a black black

beyond the possibilities of art or nature in its thrilling, glossed design, it fluttered away from (dodged) a hired man watering a team of (for some reason, harnessed and sweating) horses

alone, together, we teased around that round, full water tank, beside the windmill, in the hot sunlight, until in my teasing I glanced (I dared willfully to look)

glanced back and could not find the butterfly, only the empty air, the windmill not turning in a sky so stilled

a kind of golden dust on its wings, as if flight itself was merely ([letter no.] (5) June 26, 1991 *Revisions* n.p.)

Susan: When you were describing it, you said that there are letters we've already written and sent, and the title of it is "Revisions of Letters Already Sent." But who wrote the letters and who sent them? To whom? I think it is important to note the difference between somebody else sending letters on our behalf and our having sent letters that we're then in a position to revise. Do you see what I mean?

Robert: Yes, I see. I hadn't actually thought of that.

Susan: If my letters were "already sent"—before I was ready to send them, in my name but not of my writing—it means something quite different to come along later and be able to revise them.

Robert: I'm probably going to use that now that you've said it! That has been the case by implication, because you're right, that's a very nice distinction. Because in some of the letters, I'm interested in the pronoun that has broken loose in our time—who "you" is. There's a strain of a lover in it, but there's also arguing about poetry with someone. I've actually thought of Fred [Wah]. Sometimes I'm trying to straighten Fred out a little! But it's funny because that notion of letters already sent, you do go back to debates you had or talks you had with people and make revisions.

Susan: I guess I asked the question because I was teaching your work alongside that of Dionne Brand and Daphne Marlatt this year. And in our discussions we kept coming up against the significantly different positionings. Marlatt's work suggests that the letters have been sent for her, and that she didn't ever get to send the letters herself.

Robert: Oh no. I feel I made the mistake of sending some of the letters!

Susan: Right, and then you see what you've done. But I'm talking about not having been able to send the letter at all—not having the right postage, so to speak–that is a different position from the one you're describing.

Robert: Oh, very much so. No, I feel I wrote a lot of letters that I should have burned!

Susan: But it's a sense of seeing a different self, isn't it? A self that you don't identify with anymore?

Robert: That's right, exactly. The problem is still in my notion of self. I have the agency, so to speak. I wrote my own letters.

Pauline: You are necessarily complicit because you're part of the dominant culture; you have agency. But there's a lot of self-mockery in your work because you put yourself, the subject, out there as something that you can then critique.

Robert: Well, have you ever read that essay of mine, "I Wanted to Write a Manifesto"? In that I quote from the first poem I remember writing. It was never published. I was seventeen or eighteen and it said all the things I didn't want to say. Something was preventing me; I wasn't writing the poem, so to speak. The poem was writing me.

Susan: Were you conscious of that at the time?

Robert: Yes, I became aware of it right away.

Susan: That you felt completely frustrated because you had no way to control the language you had to write with?

Robert: Well, I did do it comically. But the poem ends, as I recall, with the death of a samurai warrior. And it said, "The wise old moon very knowingly frowned / On the man who lay sprawled on the cold grey ground. / He had taken the law of his maker in vain" (Kroetsch *A Likely Story* 52), etc. But I was vehemently against Christianity at the time. And here was the Maker, Catholic, Roman Catholic, and then there was the moon. I mean I knew you shouldn't put the moon in a poem! And I didn't know a samurai from a hole in the ground. And here when I sat down to write I wrote about a samurai warrior. And of course the verse sounds like Robert Service actually. I wanted to write a poem, and there wasn't a word of me in it. I was really baffled, I mean I wanted to write and my teacher had said, "be a writer"! And I realized I wasn't writing. And in a sense that's another one of those originary moments, if you believe in those things, where I was saying, "I have to reveal *here* somehow." But my place was nowhere in the poem.

Pauline: Does that explain why you so often set up a cultural text, or subtext, that you work with and against?

Robert: Yes I think so. I'm very attracted to subliterary texts that come out of my place, so with *Seed Catalogue* and *The Ledger* (which was my grandfather's), yes, I deliberately chose them. Or I would use the local news columns in small town newspapers where you find some of the most concentrated poems you can write: "Mrs. Jones went to Red Deer to see her new grandchild." The system of kinship and everything is stated right there in very local terms.

Pauline: I'm curious as to how your strategy of using subliterary texts works. For example, *The Ledger* gave you a structure and in *Excerpts from the Real World* you take the diary form, which implies a certain content, and then you work against it.

Robert: And also I use the Country and Western music in *Excerpts*, which I think of as very subliterary.

Pauline: You're always subverting the form too, and the clichés of the form. But I would like to talk more about the way that it's generative for you. What's your relation to that material? How do you have agency in that? To what extent is it writing you?

Robert: Well, I'm very compulsive about secrecy and concealment, I suppose. Some of those forms that announce less intention, like a postcard—its throwaway quality—enable me to be concealed and to reveal at the same time. I mean it's almost a paradox that I publish, because my real ambition is to write and never be seen.

Pauline: Is it a personal shyness? Or a way of keeping things away from your synthesizing mind? There's a part of you that knows you've got this mind that can pull everything together and so you set up these structures and say, "Okay, try that!"

Robert: You know, that is the truth. That is dead on. And I have to just keep hiding from my own systems all the time. In fact, in my war with structuralism, I mean in my fear of structuralism, it's not that I can't do it, it's...

Susan: That you can!

Pauline: How do you keep thinking up structures that will defy you?

Robert: Sometimes I fear they're going to run out on me, you know? But in "Revisions of Letters Already Sent," for example, I'm not fighting the structure. This really is my game. One of the sections will say "insert the following" and three pages later, it will say "take out the following," and it's the thing I had put in there.

Pauline: What do you pay attention to when you're working with contradictions? You're unravelling in some ways, but you're also partially putting things together.

Robert: Insofar as I'm a postcolonial writer, I have a dread of systems, because I've felt victimized by them, or erased—victim is too strong a word. I certainly wouldn't claim to speak for others. One of the things we had to do was enter into complicity. One time I was with three little Indian boys in Fort Qu'appelle and I asked them their names, which is kind of a courteous white thing to do, and they kept trading names. So, threatened by this white intruder, they shifted names. And I realized that I do the same thing when I'm threatened. And then when they asked me what I did, and I said I was a writer, the one little boy said, "Oh, my grandmother's a legender." Isn't that a great word, "legender"? I do want to tell stories for my place or culture or whatever and yet I'm uneasy about the very power that story has.

Pauline: In "Poem for My Dead Sister" (Kroetsch *A Likely Story* 157–70) you're really challenging yourself to resist the story.

Robert: Some people say I've gone too far, but I don't think so. Even Gertrude Stein, who is one of my heroes, stuck to a certain kind of grammar and vocabulary, insofar as a language is made of vocabulary and grammar. So the first thing I do is destroy grammar right off the bat. I just want the reader to know grammar won't say what I have to say. And that "Poem for My Dead Sister" was coming out of incredible pain.

Pauline: But your poems are not outside of grammar either, are they?

Robert: Well, look at the line "in the greenest of comparison" in the first part of that poem:

> 1
>
> in the greenest of comparison, water
> reads our trace against corrodibility
>
> sky is a dark virtue, whisk a word
> rinse a retrieval off the hard map
>
> klee cries, the verb retaliates,
> is isn't not enough to grieve.
>
> ("*Morning*" section of "Poem for My Dead Sister" *A Likely Story* 157–58)

I find this offensive grammatically. But I don't go as far as, say, Susan Howe does in certain of her things.

Susan: Yes, you certainly make it incomprehensible in the reading, or first reading.

Robert: In the next section the words start to come apart:

> 2
>
> timers hold eggs inside their mouths,
> if toast and word of night, a tourniquet

> winding awake, the cleavage of resistance,
> pretense of dawn, prohibit and to conjugate
>
> release, delusion of both eye and ear,
> in jest ingest, the pancake, flowered
> (*A Likely Story* 158)

Robert: And look at the "not likely" part of section four:

> 4
> the tryst of trust, calumnious
> a field of desiccated grass
>
> as is a glod in heaven
> not glikely, the rainmaker sled
>
> nor blindman's buff recoup nor
> snow hide handkerchief.
> (*A Likely Story* 159)

At the same time, look at the way the four elements appear, like I'm stuck with them. There's water and earth and, right off the bat, I'm stuck. And in my mind, by the end of the poem, I'm almost using the prairie, it's become rather specifically prairie.

Susan: The vocabulary has, yes.

Robert: Yes, or at least the imagery.

Pauline: The words here seem to be set loose and they're just spinning around. I'm curious that you're using the couplet form, which becomes a container for this swirl of words. But what generates the movement from one word to the next? You know you've got a certain length, the couplet. Do you have a rhythmic sense of how many words you can use?

Robert: It moves slowly toward almost an iambic trance by the end. And I thought of the poem as an elegy, in the sense that I'm trying to put my head together in order to deal with my sister's death. And often the words generate off sounds, the physicality of sound. Or look at the line "husk and the rind obliterate / frisk first the frosted field" in section three:

3
husk and the rind obliterate
frisk first the frosted field

branch, unbrittled, myrtle musk
hope, hope unhoping hope hoped

the bare trees, bare, the
luminosity of eye, itinerary.

("*Before the Leaves*" section of "Poem for My Dead Sister" 160)

Our notion of prettiness in language is actually based on sounds
that aren't used too much in English. Like "l" and "n." Whereas if
you look in the dictionary, "s" has got a big section! Hissing and
stuff, you know? And "f" too, like "first," "first the frosted field."

Pauline: It has an Anglo-Saxon sound to it. Alliterative.

Robert: Yes, it does. I've long been intrigued by the fact that the
earlier stage of English was alliterative.

Pauline: Do you see what you're doing here as parallel to the
Language poets?

Robert: Yes.

Pauline: But they claim a political agenda in what they're doing. Is
that part of what you're doing?

Robert: Not political in their sense. I am more specifically arguing
with the Canadian poetic establishment, which I see as incredibly
dull in certain ways. There are great poets. Fred [Wah] is one of
them. But there are masses of poets who are going along with
another stance that would be embarrassing in any other part of
the English-speaking world, except maybe Australia!

Pauline: So this is as anti-lyric as you can get. In fact there isn't an
"I" in here at all.

Robert: You can trace this back. There's that poem of mine that has
no pronouns whatsoever, "The Criminal Intensities of Love as
Paradise" (*Completed Field Notes* 81–95) where I just said, "I
can't handle pronouns anymore." But here, there's no "I."

Pauline: How does the couplet work for you?

Robert: I found the couplet very generative. Using the verse form
was a way to contain my grief, and then of course, against that,
using funny or bad puns. Even Dennis Cooley was offended that I

would laugh and make bad jokes about death, and he's a very far-out poet. Even the day my sister was dying, we would laugh. My sister's daughter was there, she was laughing. The release of laughter is just incredible.

Susan: In these poems it seems you're interrogating language at the level of sound and word, instead of discourse.

Robert: Yes that's right. When I announced at the end of *Completed Field Notes* that I was finished writing poetry, I felt I had run out of ways to subvert myself. And the irony of this poem is, I was under incredible stress, and (this was in California) I had never used a computer. My sister lived with a woman [Eleanor] very close to us and I was sitting at her computer, trying to figure out how to use it. And I tried by writing a poem about my sister.

Susan: This poem?

Robert: No not this, but I wrote a couple of lines, and it was coming out as just jumble. And the phone rang, and said "Rush to the hospital, your sister's dying." And I had to actually write later to Eleanor and say, "could you give me a copy of what I wrote on your computer." Isn't this awful in the presence of death? I had to say to her, "I was playing on the computer. Would you send me what that was?" So she sent me a copy. And I said, "There's a possibility in that...." It gave me a way to start.

Susan: I find it interesting that, although there are no pronouns, you call this a poem "for *my* dead sister," not "*the poet's* dead sister," as you did in "The Poet's Mother" (*Completed Field Notes* 206–9), for example. Using "the poet's" rather than "my" distances the reader much more from the speaker of the poem.

Robert: Okay, I like that. I don't remember having thought about the pronouns. Certainly, you know, one of my wars has been with that word "poet," because I was given such a high-falutin' notion of the word "poet," it paralysed me.

Pauline: Except for Robert Service?

Robert: Yes. And I liked him because he did subvert—you know people used to make fun of his poems, they don't so much anymore. And I used to think seriously, secretly to myself, "I kind of like those poems, you know?"

Pauline: Susan and I were talking the other day about how criticism of your work has often focussed on what you're undoing and resisting but rarely focuses on the things that you're affirming.

I think your work is affirmative in a very interesting way. It affirms the ordinary, the banal, the everyday, the earth and water, which come in constantly, much more than, say, the sky and all that celestial stuff.

Robert: Oh, very much so.

Pauline: Would you call that a mythology?

Robert: Cosmology might be a more useful word, because a myth is really a story that talks about the cosmos.

Pauline: There's an affirmation in your work of a whole realm of experience that isn't affirmed, particularly in a colonial society, which takes its structures from elsewhere. I don't know to what extent you're conscious of that.

Robert: Sure, very much, I think of myself as comic, but not in the playwright sense of comic; comic in the sense of excessive. Or supplementary. Any of those ideas, because excess overrides the paradigm, even a cosmology. And you can't argue inside the cosmology and win; it's got you beat, in that sense. They've explained you already, like when I was a kid. But over and over every cosmology that gets defeated is defeated by excess. I mean, you say that the earth is at the centre of the system, and pretty soon there's too much evidence, so you say it must be the sun. You get too much evidence. There is always something in excess of whatever system. That's what I want. That's why I document the sub-literary.

Pauline: And the banal, and the clichéd, you work a lot with clichés.

Robert: That's what I was doing in *The Sad Phoenician*. All of the clichés we use to construct ourselves have a validity. If I say to myself, "I'm a good guy," I might in some way have to follow my own dictum, you know? I'd have to at least be a good guy now and then. And you can't escape it after a while. I was much taken to hear that in warrior cultures in Africa, when they sing the praise of the leader, part of the function of the song is to put the bastard on the spot. So it wasn't just idle, false praise. It had a political intention too.

Susan: That interests me, too. I think about the difference between you speaking the banal, the domestic, the ordinary, the everyday, and what happens when women writers do so. In a sense, after you have argued for the value of the everyday, once you've given it a kind of validity, it has an authority that it otherwise doesn't have. But when a woman writer does the same thing, she is not seen as able to confer authority or value. And that's partly because you have authority as a poet—dare I say a high-falutin' poet—if you see what I mean.

Robert: Yes, you're quite right. I have demonstrated that if I want to write high-falutin' stuff I can do it.

Susan: To have the privilege of being able to value the domestic, that is a privilege you have only if that's not all that is expected from you.

Robert: I couldn't agree more. That's right.

Pauline: For a man, entering that domestic space is entering an area of excess.

Robert: That's a perfect example because we have a very tight paradigm of "male," at least in our culture. And you load it up, and I say, "I like to iron my own shirts." Something as simple as that becomes a form of excess.

Susan: But the difference is that once a woman tries to articulate the banal, the everyday, and the ordinary, what she's articulating in the first instance is its oppressiveness. What she might need to do first is critique, not celebrate it. And that's a big difference.

Robert: Okay, but in literature, though, one example I can think of a woman achieving this excess is say Molly Bloom at the end of *Ulysses*. And her excess overwhelms Leopold Bloom's paradigm. She has lots of lovers, and she's thinking about good oral sex at the end, and her sense of language and so on…it does stay in a certain way domestic and banal. But she brings in much more, doesn't she? What you're saying is very central in the predicament of the woman poet.

Susan: Yes, I was speaking of women poets, not women characters in texts written by men, since the domestic can never be celebrated in an uncomplicated way by a woman, because it's also a place of such oppression.

Robert: I know, you're quite right. In fact, you see women poets who try to do this, even squirming themselves a bit as they talk about it. I am aware that I'm still trading off of a certain paradigm of male poet. I am, and I can't get around it.

Susan: I am interested in the ways that you foreground the structures that limit and define and exclude certain experiences. I think a lot of your work does take on gender as a structure. But have you done that deliberately? Has that been a structure you have wanted to take on or not?

Robert: You have to read my next novel *The Puppeteer* since it's all about asking the question: Who is the puppet?

Pauline: But what does that have to do with gender roles?

Robert: Well it has to do with many things, including gender. But I am asking who controls narrative? The wedding dress itself becomes a very powerful narrator. So yes, I think I have been aware of gender since I was a kid because I wasn't willing to go with the male model, or with the men. I didn't like the goddamn work I had to do, for one thing! And then I had hay fever, which excluded me from some very male activities. But my second sister especially would go out and work, and I had an incredible uneasiness that she was out there working and here I was sitting in the house reading a book. So the notion of gender was problematic for me very early. As well, I had sisters and no brothers, so I had curious role models. In an extended family of that sort, the women were very powerful and were at home, while the men worked long hours in the fields.

Pauline: The women had the dominant position in a certain sphere. But in terms of the larger social structure, the men still occupied the privileged positions.

Robert: I'm not quarrelling with that for a minute, no.

Pauline: But in your poems where there is a lover and a love-object, or even in the mother poems, there is a sense of gendered positions, particularly for the speaker. I realize that you often critique constructions of masculinity. But are you conscious of the ways you participate in it, or is it more that you're conscious of the female presence?

Robert: I see the end of that first poem to my mother* as—well, I become her approaching lover, which is very male, the impregnator. Smaro [Kamboureli] was quite offended when she first looked at that poem, because that was almost immoral in a sense. Let me just circle around. One of the problems is that one works by parody at first, and to work with parody is not really to destroy or to change the paradigm.

---

* "The Poet's Mother" (*Completed Field Notes* 206).

Susan: It doesn't take you to any other place. It doesn't offer alternatives. For example, a student of mine just wrote a paper comparing the metaphors of sexuality in your essay "For Play and Entrance" with Nicole Brossard's *Under Tongue*. While your piece clearly works with a male model of sexual experience—even if it does so parodically—Brossard's not only doesn't concern itself with critique or even parody; it moves immediately to the configuration of alternatives.

Robert: Well I'm very much caught—I hate to admit it—in the quest paradigm, even though I treat it very parodically. And the quest is male in a certain way. I mean, whether it's hunting a woman to go to bed with or looking for the Holy Grail.

Susan: Maybe that's one structure you haven't felt the need to break out of?

Robert: Or even more cynically, if you are a large, white, male, who has learned how to make himself attractive to women…

Susan: It's not exactly in your interest to get rid of that paradigm, right?

Pauline: Another way to come at this involves asking whether there is an ethics of postmodernism.

Robert: Well, one tends to flinch at the word now because ethics seems anathema to postmodernism. My sense is that some critics of postmodernism assume that ethics must be linked to particular paradigms, requiring writers to stay within the limits of those paradigms. To say that I'm a "comic" writer is to suggest that I shouldn't be taken seriously, instead of setting up comedy against something else like tragedy, which I think is a much bigger fake than comedy ever was.

Pauline: Do you see yourself as having an ethical position?

Robert: I think of myself as incredibly ethical. I mean, I have just an appalling difficulty even using violence in fiction—the kind of physical or psychological violence that are the stock and trade of popular culture.

Pauline: Does your parody come from a moral position?

Robert: Yes I think parody often comes from a moral position. You're trying to indicate "this is wrong" by putting sugar on the pill. There's a hidden ethicist in me!

Pauline: Which writers in Canada would you consider particularly interesting in terms of these questions?

Robert: Fred [Wah] and George [Bowering] are two of the most ethical writers around, and I would put myself with them in a certain way because we take literary form so seriously. To take literary form seriously is to say, this is a reflection of everything else. You cannot, out of nowhere, write, or use a form. In the eighteenth century people wrote couplets for one hundred years. It's mind-boggling to us, but it was a form that was enabling them to say everything they had to say about the culture, you see. Or blank verse, Shakespeare's blank verse; he didn't have to try another verse form. That verse form was saying what they had to say in the culture. And I think so many poets—I really get irked by Canadian poets—are using dead forms. And they cannot say anything.

Pauline: Do you think the term "postmodern" is still useable?

Robert: Well, I tend to avoid it myself, but...

Susan: What word would you use to describe the writing that interests you?

Robert: I think we're stuck with "Postmodern" as both a stance and a period in the way that, say, "Romanticism" is both a stance and a period. There were all kinds of other writers around during the Romantic period, but the Romantics won the day in some canonical way. You could, I'm sure, go and unearth some very good writing that had nothing to do with Romanticism. I think the present is going to be seen, however briefly, as a Postmodern period. And just as, when I was a graduate student, there were about 300 definitions of "Romanticism" there must be up to about 300 now for postmodernism.

Pauline: If we're going to historicize this thirty-year period, 1960–1990, perhaps that's going to have to be the term.

Robert: One of the problems is that to give this writing a different name would be to position it outside. And the postmodern is so involved in so many disciplines, in so many countries. No, I don't think there's a way around it for the moment.

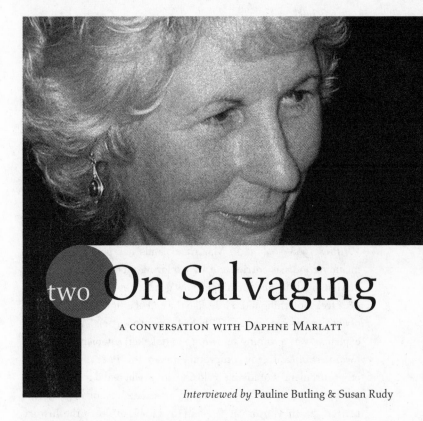

two On Salvaging

A CONVERSATION WITH DAPHNE MARLATT

Interviewed by Pauline Butling & Susan Rudy

DAPHNE MARLATT [BUCKLE] IS A POET, NOVELIST, THEORIST, EDITOR, essayist, and teacher from Vancouver. Born in Melbourne, Australia in 1942, she lived in Penang, Malaysia from 1945 until 1951, when the family immigrated to Vancouver. Marlatt majored in English and Creative Writing at the University of British Columbia (B.A. 1964). At UBC she became a member of the second editorial group of TISH: *A Poetry Newsletter, Vancouver* (1963–64), studied creative writing with Robert Creeley, took Warren Tallman's Studies in Poetry course, and studied with Charles Olson at the 1963 Summer Poetry Workshop. In 1968, she completed an M.A. in Comparative Literature at the University of Indiana with a translation of Frances Ponge. In 1996, she received an LLD from the University of Western Ontario and in 2004, an honorary degree from Mount Saint Vincent, Nova Scotia.

Marlatt's 40 year publication history demonstrates an exceptionally wide range of interests and an innovative approach to genre. She transforms traditional narrative and poetic forms with creative uses of autobiography, travelogue, journal, fictional narrative, oral history, and/or translation. Marlatt's work is groundbreaking thematically as well as formally. In all her writing she challenges gender constructs, explores outsider experiences, and exposes forms of oppression and exclusion. Her first book, *Frames of a Story* (1968), together with numerous publications in the 1970s, show Marlatt experimenting with language and form and questioning social formations. In *leaf leaf/s* (1969), the poems track a restless consciousness leafing out as it interacts with the world: "I started living my own life. My phrase for it was 'taking on more ground.' I wanted to feel that I had a right to live in a world" ("Given This Body" 55–56). In *Rings* (1971) and *What Matters: Writing 1968–70* (1980), Marlatt expands her poetic ground by including journal entries and by exploring taboo subjects such as marital break-up and birthing: "Now gently, now hardly push at all. / & i feel something like a loss, like the end of a sigh, / A cry, a squall of absolute protest, pain?" (*What Matters* 100–101). "At issue" she explains, "was a coming to own up to (take on) my place in a world i was part of & already compromised in. & this in & through those other turbulences of loving & 'losing' love (where did it go?), of first mothering, & of finding a voice to articulate any of it" ("Of the matter" 7). In *Vancouver Poems* (1972), she explores the history and mythology of place, as constructed by and in language. In the highly successful *Steveston* (with photographer Robert Minden 1974), a response to the everyday lives and declining fortunes of the Japanese Canadian fishermen in the coastal town of Steveston near Vancouver, Marlatt develops a fluid, prose-poem line that accommodates a complex blend of local history, social critique, and phenomenological awareness. In *Zócalo* (1977), an autobiographical travelogue of a trip to Mexico and in "In the Month of Hungry Ghosts" (1979), a travel narrative in the form of letters and poems written during a trip to Penang, she again creates hybrid forms that combine lyric, narrative, autobiographical, and critical impulses. During the 1970s, Marlatt edited two publications based on local, aural histories: *Steveston Recollected: a Japanese-Canadian History* (with M. Koizumi, 1975) and *Opening Doors: Vancouver's East End* (with Carol Itter, 1980), the latter book developing out of her work as an oral historian with the British Columbia Provincial Archives. She also served as poetry editor of *The Capilano Review* (1973–76) and co-founded (with Paul de Barros) *periodics: a magazine of prose* (1977–81). A selection of Marlatt's writing from the 1960s and 1970s is collected in *Net Work: Selected Writing* (1980). Her two travel narratives from the 1970s, together with *How Hug a Stone* (1983) about a trip to England with her son Kit, were later republished in *Ghost Works* (1993).

In the 1980s, Marlatt's focus shifted to exploring feminist theory, forming ties with women's communities (especially Nicole Brossard and other feminist writers in Quebec), and articulating a lesbian erotic. She published two groundbreaking collections of lesbian love poems, *Touch to My Tongue* (1984) and *Double Negative*, with Betsy Warland (1988), followed by *Salvage* (1991), which includes revisions of earlier work that recover suppressed feminist concerns: "I was blocked and I couldn't see my way out because I didn't have the theory that would have helped me do that" (Interview with Williamson 182). Her collaborations with Betsy Warland were republished as *Two Women in a Birth* (1994). Other collaborative projects include *Mauve* (1985) and *character/jeu de letters* (1986) with Nicole Brossard.

Her community-building work has included taking on the job of Program Coordinator for the Women & Words/les femmes et les mots conference in Vancouver in 1983, starting the feminist journal *Tessera* in 1985 (with Barbara Godard, Kathy Mezei, and Gail Scott), and organizing a conference for lesbian women in 1989, which led to the co-edited publication (with Sky Lee, Lee Maracle, and Betsy Warland) *Telling It: Women and Language Across Cultures* (1990). *Readings from the Labyrinth* (1998) collects her critical essays from a 20 year period, beginning with the feminist classic, "musing with mothertongue," first presented as a paper at the Dialogue conference at York University in 1981. In the late 1980s and 1990s, Marlatt produced two critically acclaimed novels, *Ana Historic* (1988) and *Taken* (1996), and is currently at work on a third. She continues to write poetry, publishing *This Tremor Love Is* in 2001, "an album of love poems spanning twenty-five years" (back cover). Here Marlatt continues the process that she began in *Salvage* of revising earlier poems and/or recontextualizing them by placing them alongside current work. Following the thread of memory, the poems explore the "tremors" of desire, pleasure, anguish, and ecstasy that accompany love and loss. The first section, "A Lost Book," spans 25 years and ranges from a poem for Marlatt's mother, "here is a table we sit to where our hands rest or move [/] as the words speak out of their separate quiet" (17), to love poems—"nouns i want to call you   winter/rice/tea strain, unlikely [/] sweet tongue, a green hope i bury my face into" (11)—to anguished moments: "torn between. two yous.   to you & you, from the used heart, the over- [/] exposed, petals fallen" (30). The second section ("Here and There") combines recent work with some poems from Marlatt's 1981 chapbook *here & there*. "Impossible Portraiture" (the fourth section) is a sequence of love poems "for Bridget." The fifth and final section ("Tracing the Cut") meditates on the tropes of presence and absence in the presence of such natural wonders as "the splendour of light's appetite / eating up detail in this /dark fist of mountains" (103) and in the grip of "ravenous, ponderous... [//] ghosts and gods [that] throng the / familial body" (109). Language provides connections, "opens its connect- / ing points, com- / panion in this eating of light" (104); and at the end the poet is at peace, "sitting simply," with "wind-, lake-, pine- /mothers all round" (110).

Daphne Marlatt has taught numerous writing workshops; served as Writer in Residence at the Universities of Alberta, Winnipeg, Saskatchewan, Western Ontario, Windsor, and Simon Fraser University; and has been a senior writing instructor at the Banff School of Fine Arts. In 2002 she was appointed adjunct instructor at Simon Fraser University.

Her fiction, poetry, and essays have been published in numerous magazines. She has been anthologized in *Modern Canadian Stories* (ed. Rimanelli 1966), *New Wave Canada* (ed. Souster 1966), *The Long Poem Anthology* (ed. Ondaatje 1979), *The New Long Poem Anthology* (ed. Thesen 1991 and 2001), *The New Oxford Book of Canadian Verse* (ed. Atwood 1982), *Poetry by Canadian Women* (ed. Sullivan 1989), *Making a Difference: Canadian Multicultural Literature* (ed. Kamboureli 1996), *Uncommon Wealth: An Anthology of Poetry in English* (ed. Besner et al. 1997), *15 Canadian Poets x 3* (ed. Geddes 4th edition 2001), and *A New Anthology of Canadian Literature in English* (eds. Bennett and Brown 2002). For critical discussions of her poetry, see Barbara Godard, "Body I: Daphne Marlatt's Feminist Poetics"; Janice Williamson, "'It gives me a great deal of pleasure to say yes': Reading/Writing Lesbian in Daphne Marlatt's *Touch to My Tongue*; Neuman and Kamboureli (eds.), "A Special Daphne Marlatt Feature," *Line* 13 (1989); Julie Beddoes,

"Mastering the Mother Tongue: Reading Frank Davey Reading Daphne Marlatt's *How Hug a Stone*"; Douglas Barbour, *Daphne Marlatt and Her Works*; Miriam Nichols, "Subjects of Experience: Post-cognitive Subjectivity in the Work of bpNichol and Daphne Marlatt"; Pauline Butling, "'From Radical to Integral': Daphne Marlatt's 'Booking Passage'"; Susan Knutson, *Narrative in the Feminine: Daphne Marlatt and Nicole Brossard*; and Sabrina Reed, "'Against the Source': Daphne Marlatt's Revision of Charles Olson."

—PB

Pauline Butling: We're interested in talking about the writing process in *Salvage.* The title suggests you have a definite purpose in writing the book, which is to "salvage" earlier work. What is the relation between that goal and your commitment to open form and process in your writing? How do you combine intention and receptivity? Is that too complicated to start off with?

Daphne Marlatt: It's pretty complicated. Quite apart from the notion of audience, there are two things going on here in terms of intent. There's the intent that gets established in the editing, and there's the intent that develops in the writing of the individual pieces. This is an unusual book for me because it was put together without being written with the concept of the whole.

Pauline: When did you decide on the title?

Daphne: When I started working with the idea of salvaging those original *Steveston* poems. It really came up in "Litter, Wreckage, Salvage" and I shortened it to *Salvage* for the title of the book. I knew then that what I was going to do was put together work that was scattered, salvage it from just fading away and put it into some work where the poems could function together until I'd winnowed out what didn't seem to quite fit. It was only in the course of doing that that I began to see what shape it would take, and I don't mean just formal shape. I mean signifying shape as well. It was by going through the process of putting these things together that I could see what it was thematically. All the manifestations of "passages" as a motif became clear to me when I was typing out the table of contents. Which was when I started doing the section titles.

But that's just the editorial level. On the writing level, that's where it gets interesting because this book includes writing that was started almost twenty years ago, much of which was radically transformed. I imagine it would be like painting over an old canvas where you're painting over figures that are already there and at the same time you're uncovering some of them. There's that Matisse painting where the figures are dancing around the table and you see these shadow figures under the figures that are already there.

Pauline: But in the painting over, or uncovering, you're looking for certain things?

Daphne: Yes, that begins to develop in the process. I don't want to start with that intention because I really want to let each poem begin to show me where it's going. If I know what my intent is before I start writing, I'm bored; the piece just dies, so I'm the kind of writer that needs to let the writing slowly manifest itself.

Pauline: So the intention "to write in lesbian" (*Salvage* 118), which is clearly articulated by the end of the book, was not necessarily present from the beginning? It becomes clear to you by the end of the book?

Daphne: That's exactly how it happened.

Pauline: You didn't begin with the intention of looking for the concealed and/or emerging female experience?

Daphne: That is an intention through all my work, but it's a very general intention. It doesn't get honed until the particular piece makes clear to me what version of that is manifesting itself. It has always been important for me to write out of my experience as a woman because I felt that was the unspeakable, the ignored, the elided. I wanted to make it present in the same way as the TISH group of writers wanted to make Vancouver present. There was this sense that this place was unwritten and should be on the map and I had that same sense about female experience. That's why I was writing about giving birth and nursing and adolescent sexual conditioning.

Pauline: You've become so much more politicised in recent years. How does political context affect the writing?

Daphne: This brings out a much larger issue, which is exactly the issue of audience and community you asked about.

Pauline: But not just audience in terms of who you're writing for, but also how the community informs your writing.

Daphne: Exactly. Exactly. I'm thinking of that term Nicole [Brossard] uses—"*rapport d'adresse*"— and Gail Scott uses it too. It's like a two-way street. For me the strongest evidence for it is when I'm actually standing before an audience reading. It never feels one-way. I always get a sense of what's coming back to me from the audience. Reading a piece is the surest way for me to hear it critically because I can hear what is working and what is not working—now that's an immediate thing.

On a larger scale, part of my politicization obviously comes from the reading that I've done in feminist theory over the years and the sense of having a community of women writers whose work I admire. I want to be part of that dialogue. That happens on a solitary level, on a reading level, and on a public level. It's a result of all the readings I've given over the years and the feedback I've got, especially from women in the audience who come up and say that's exactly what happened to me or, that's exactly how I felt, or it's like touching a raw nerve. You have the corroboration that your experience is not singular, solitary. It's part of a whole spectrum of female experience. What is so exciting is getting this articulated and out so we can talk to each other, and others. Men, who constitute the malestream, the mainstream, have to take cognition of it, they have to take account of it, it's there, it's out there.

Pauline: Does your awareness of this female community and culture empower the "I" in the poem?

Daphne: "I" was not a problem for me. "We" was a problem for a long time. Whether I had the right to say "we." White middle class women's experience was made to represent all of women's experience and it just doesn't work because there are so many differences among us. So then I became more conscious of that "we" and tried to root it in a more personal "we." For instance, when I write "we" in "Booking Passage" (*Salvage* 115–19) it starts off with a "we" of Betsy [Warland] and me, it's rooted in that "I-you" dialogue and then it begins to enlarge, but it enlarges in the context of that lesbian tradition.

Pauline: When you bring in Sappho and others I feel that "we" begins to include the reader too (*Salvage* 119).

Daphne: Yes, yes, I hope it does.

Pauline: Another thing I want to talk about is your use of the prose poem in *Salvage* and the question of genre blurring. Marjorie Perloff in her introduction to *Postmodern Genres* suggests postmodern texts work by installing a genre in order to contest it (8). Do you set up a tension between prose and poetry?

Daphne: That works nicely with feminist thought because the forms and the language that we've inherited don't quite fit, there's always a subversion going on or a contesting.

Pauline: I find your use of the prose poem forces more attention to the horizontal language axis and puts words into metonymic relation, in contrast to the lyric form which torques the line in interesting ways but mostly on a vertical (metaphoric) axis.

Daphne: Well the tension in a short-line poem is between the torquing of the line and the continuation of the discursive. In a prose poem you're working with a sentence, and it's a sentence that's very loose, it can gather all kinds of stuff into it, because in English we're not so driven by the Latinate declinations to indicate grammatical connections. English rests much more on position. You can put things side by side and they have a very loose connection with a capacity for meaning-play and that's how I like to build my sentences; that's why I play around with the resources of punctuation like commas, dashes and brackets. Those are the ones I principally use. An English sentence has a tremendous capacity for detour, and that's what's pulled me further and further into prose.

Pauline: In the English sentence, the functions aren't fixed. They depend on the position and environment of the word.

Daphne: And sometimes the meaning will change radically just on the basis of position alone, where you're balancing what comes before and what comes after in a run-on effect.

Pauline: Does the un-covering and dis-covering of meanings work better for you in the prose poem?

Daphne: Yes, I came to feel very restricted in verse form. I suppose it's partly because my lines were so short, and that was the influence of [Louis] Zukofsky and [Robert] Creeley and [Cid] Corman.

Pauline: There was a notion of words as palpable, even a preciousness that seemed fun for a while.

Daphne: I know, I know but then I got impatient with that and thought okay, I would write lines as long as the margins of a conventional prose text on a standard $8^{1}/_{2}$ by 11 inch page. That was interesting because that brought me bang up against punctuation.

Pauline: Punctuation becomes the equivalent of the line break?

Daphne: That's right. How I was going to score the rhythms I was hearing became a crucial factor because I wanted them to be read the way I was hearing them. So that was a very good lesson for me in scoring as well as the critical part that punctuation plays. But then I got tired of having to negotiate the end of the line at the right margin. It began to seem too arbitrary. At first it was fun to play around with the arbitrariness, it was a challenge, whether I could keep it going, but then I got tired of it because it began to get in the way. I suppose what I was reaching for was more and more space to invade my prose and that's what's beginning to happen with the breaks in those long stanzagraphs in *Steveston.*

Pauline: What do you mean by stanzagraph?

Daphne: A combination of a paragraph and a stanza. I can't remember now who gave me that term but it feels right. What looks like a prose paragraph but isn't because it's composed of long lines—this will break and then there'll be part of a long line hung in space, followed by another long stanzagraph. What I wanted was a sense of flow down the page from one group of lines to the next, the way thought, perception, flows—sometimes fast, sometimes slow but not rationally organized the way a paragraph normally is. Later I began to be interested in what happens when you hang everything off the left margin, as in a list, and that's partly how "Booking Passage" is built. A list descends down a page but it isn't one sentence running on and on, it's more fragmented, composed more of discreet connections and perceptions. "Booking Passage" is prose that goes to the right-hand margin, but in smaller units. In the stanzagraphs in *Steveston* there's a sense of this long continual flow that's winding down and down. In "Booking Passage" I wanted more a sense of a series, of beginning and rebeginning to articulate something.

Pauline: Let's look at the opening stanzagraph of "Booking Passage"—is that what you're talking about?

Daphne: Yes. The way these units of the poem are quite short—they interrupt each other, for instance: "i nose the book aside and pull you / forward gently with my lips"—that is the end of one unit. I'll read both units and then you can see the difference:

> passage booked. i see you by the window shore slips by,
> you reading Venice our history is, that sinking feel, those
> footings under water. i nose the book aside and pull you
> gently forward with my lips.

> a path, channel or duct. a corridor. a book and not a book.
> not *booked* but off the record. this.

> irresistible melt of hot flesh. furline and thawline align
> your long wet descent.
> (*Salvage* 116)

In a sense there's an interruption at the end of each of the units and I was really interested in how that worked.

Pauline: Each unit flows out from that left-hand margin—to begin and re-begin.

Daphne: That's part of the poem's erotic movement, a sense of coming and coming and coming.

Pauline: You said earlier that in the prose poem you work mainly with the sentence. Do you have a definition of a sentence?

Daphne: I have more of a sense of what a sentence isn't. I'm more interested in undermining the conventional notions of sentences, so I use a lot of sentence fragments.

Pauline: But they don't feel like fragments to you, do they?

Daphne: No, a fragment suggests something split off. My sense of it is more organic, it's always connected, no matter how loosely, and it's a beginning that doesn't end with an end; it initiates something further.

Pauline: Is it a rhythmic unit then?

Daphne: Yes it's partly rhythmic, a period partly indicates a point of rest in the movement of thought, but that's only temporary because then the next movement happens and it's often reflecting back on the preceding one. My favourite image for this is time-lapse photography where you're looking at a branch growing and you may do this over a period of three or four days if you take a photograph every few hours or so. But when you look at the film it looks as if the branch is growing non-stop. That's how I feel a sentence works.

Pauline: Do you use the sentence as a means of integrating, even forcing things together? As a unit that can make words interact with each other, get along with each other in a way they might not have otherwise? Is it a container in any way?

Daphne: I don't think of it as a container and I have trouble with the word forcing. I think that the extreme tension that can be created by the collision of certain kinds of autonomy probably happens for me around the periods and the periods can be used rather dramatically for this.

Pauline: Does the period mark an ending?

Daphne: It just indicates a momentary resting place, it's a point of growth and at that point thought can take off in various directions, though of course it's shaped by the next word that follows the period which will then shape the sequence of words which follows it, which will in that sense determine the—I don't want to say sentence—the unit, the constellation of words you end up with.

Pauline: A sensorium?

Daphne: That's a lovely word. I used it in a poem once because I had this Olson sense of it as somehow indicating the endless interplay between our sensory system and all that surrounds us ("At Birch Bay").

Pauline: I don't think we can quite talk about the sentence as a sensorium.

Daphne: No, because unfortunately we are locked into the linear through grammar.

Pauline: We still read one word after the other, where the idea of the sensorium is that all these things happen at one time.

Daphne: Yes, and I love that tension between the linear movement of narrative. The conventional sentence is narrative and attempts to undermine it, divert it.

Pauline: Some critics have commented on the extreme binary oppositions in your work. You have been criticized as essentialist, falling into the old models, but it seems to me that if there are oppositions, you work with them in a creative tension. The binary oppositions are cultural and you can't pretend they don't exist, so instead of ignoring them, you work with the tension, you increase the tension, to subvert and disrupt them.

Daphne: Yes, I talk quite a bit about that in the interview with Brenda Carr ("Between Continuity and Difference") and our conversation about the margin and the centre. For me, the writing doesn't go anywhere without some form of tension. I'm always after that in some way when I'm writing, and the process of opposites interrelating. We talk about binary oppositions as something we want to get rid of but binaries are actually embedded in the function or definition that language itself performs, so they've become a function of the way we think. Binaries have also become so formulated, so frozen, in rational thought—which is the dominant mode we've inherited—I'm quite at a loss for words somehow to counteract that. I know writing out of my body counteracts it, but I don't know if I can define the strategies for writing out of my body, I don't know if I can describe what it feels like. The thinking that happens in this writing is definitely a radiating kind of thinking, not a linear kind of thinking. It's not this—and—then—this—and—therefore—this, it's much more interested in connecting in diverse ways. Nicole [Brossard] uses the image of the spiral, which is a useful metaphor. I tend to think more in terms of a network like a neural network when you get different patches firing at different moments, but they're also connected. A tension gets built up and the tension has to do with giving equal weight to the different patches, not trying to prioritize them and put them into some kind of hierarchy of value. That seems to be at the root of what I mean by writing out of the body.

Pauline: Has your sense of writing out of the body changed much? You used to talk about it in terms of proprioception and phenomenology.

Daphne: Which never took into account gender difference. We're all supposed to have these pseudo male bodies. So yes, it has. And now it's further complicated by the nature/culture critique. If you talk about the body you run the risk of being labelled right away as essentialist.

Pauline: Would you talk about the gender differences in writing out of the body that you've become aware of? How has that changed your writing process?

Daphne: Well, the body seems definitely affected by how we think of it. Our culture sets up male and female in such a way that perhaps it's easier for women to be in touch with the shifting, cyclical nature of our bodies, while men are taught to ignore the subtle cycles of their own bodies. It seems to me the male sense is of a more stable body—at least until aging sets in. But the youthful sense of the body is of a more stable, dependable substance. Women's bodies are always doing unpredictable things—bleeding, getting pregnant, getting all kinds of autoimmune disorders and so on. So where a man tends to feel the body is more a launching pad for his actions, a woman has to somehow live with or live within her body and perhaps more uneasily. I'll take a leap here and say that for me that has something to do with writing. There's a willingness to swim in the drift of language as a body, even to get lost in it, and not want to dive into certain conclusions.

[In the middle of the previous comments, Fred Wah enters the room and joins the conversation.]

Daphne: Well Fred, what do you think of all that?

Fred Wah: I think that's partly true, the male uses the body as a thing to push off from. But, for me, the feeling of the body in writing is of literally embodying a flow, a musical flow. It's not just pushing off from, it's a being within. In fact for me, in my life, writing's one of the few times I'm able to get in touch with my body. Language as motion, emotional layers within the writing.

Daphne: Definitely. I think sounds affect our bodies, in fact very old oral cultures still know that about chanting, know that certain sounds produce certain effects on the body, and we've lost touch with that.

Fred: I know that since the "voice" debate started I'm consciously trying to look at (particularly in *Diamond Grill*, this biologue

I'm working on) what maleness is, because the father thing just won't go away, it's become very strong. I've been trying to find that in the syntax, or in the words, and the way phrases come together. I haven't been able to locate it, that gendered voice for myself, there. I know that you can take a chunk of text and you can say that this is situated culturally and is gendered, depending where the text speaks to, what images are involved and so forth. But the nitty-gritty of one word after the next word, in that kind of language work, I haven't been able to locate it. If I decide to use a strong verb rather than a passive verb, for example, is that gendered?

Daphne: No, that's too simple. I think gender is only one of the markers that operates, and the other ones are more obvious so that's what we pick up on first, like class, like race, or culture which is perhaps even more pervasive. I'm trying to do what you're trying to do Fred—I love your word biologue—I'm trying to do that with my parents too, but I'm finding their cultural world—marked by just a few words of Malay that they used to use naturally in their conversation—is a place that is stronger even than gender difference.

Fred: But I would think that if anyone's going to find out, be able to locate this in our English, it will be someone like you and will certainly be a woman, someone who's working consciously trying to disentangle the gendered language constructs. I was thinking you of all people should sense this in translating Nicole. If there's a gendered voice speaking to me, it's definitely Nicole Brossard.

Daphne: What do you mean by a gendered voice in Nicole?

Fred: Well specifically when she takes the "fl" out of "fluid" and makes it the last word in the poem ("Articulation" *Daydream Mechanics* 63). When I first saw that, it was so, embodying— only something she could do. The whole piece was a struggle to articulate a sense of the body, in that instance the sense of the body being a river, and it wasn't coming from just playing with language like I might stumble across such a fragmentation.

Daphne: It comes out of a female erotic, and that's why I think of her voice as pre-eminently a lesbian voice. It's not just that sound, it's everything that sound comes to represent in the whole piece.

Fred: But isn't lesbian a gendered voice?

Daphne: If it is, where would we put it in the usual binary gender system? It's not feminine in the way we've come to define the heterosexual feminine.

Fred: Would it be more useful to think of a sexualized voice. There might be more to find out in the language by looking at it that way, because sexuality certainly has a physical basis in desire.

Daphne: And desire—what is evoked in the body in the act of making love—can change. I know that my lesbian body is different erotically from my heterosexual body.

Fred: We enact gender, we take on those roles, but I don't think that from within my body I act man. I act sexually man—that involves a whole bunch of drives. Gender doesn't seem to me to be a movement; it seems to be simply a consistency.

Daphne: There are further complications in all of this. I don't think that you can say that everything to do with the sexual functions of a woman's body are sexual. Giving birth is not only sexual—it has a sexual component—but it's not only sexual; nor is breast feeding or menstruating. Then there's also the whole cultural thing in terms of desire, what turns you on. It's the one area considered to be the least coded because it's in the realm of the personal, and there isn't an armouring around it the way there is about sex and gender.

Fred: Well, the armouring around it is pornography. When does the erotic become pornographic?

Daphne: Yes, right. But again that's in terms of reading. That's not in terms of production. My poems would be considered pornographic in certain circles.

Fred: I think the reading is more gendered than the writing.

Daphne: Well, I'm really interested in the spiritual right now, which is an impossible term to talk about, because I think the spiritual may be actually where we transcend gender. It has to do with pure awareness, not locked into time and place in the material. It's very, very difficult to bring across into language, which is always locked into the material.

Fred: I think you're right on. This is a term that was shelved some fifteen years ago. It's a term we need to go back to, I agree, and I think along with that term there are all kinds of aspects, of qualifiers like purity, the pure and the impure, a whole different discourse when you bring that up. We're forgetting a major thing, at least for us, for the literary milieu that we came out of, the Duncanness [Robert Duncan], the lush, full possibility in the world. How to be in the world spiritually. I think it's a term that would be useful for those of us who come out of the sixties, because a lot of that was around then.

Daphne: It's there in George [Bowering] but very masked, just read *Kerrisdale Elegies*.

Susan Rudy: Can you talk about what you mean by "spiritual"?

Daphne: It's so difficult to talk about. I have to think about it some more before I can venture trying to embody it, or put it into words, which, because language is set up that way, always cuts off a part of it.

Susan: In the letter you wrote me a couple of months ago you were talking about memory and coming apart at the seams, and I was thinking about that in relation to salvage, the selvedge of the fabric, or the seaming that's there.

Daphne: Well that's to prevent unravelling.

Susan: The selvedge (self-edge) prevents the unravelling and I was wondering if you could talk about memory in relation to this book, the relation of memory and salvage and what decisions you make, what's salvaged, where the self's edge is.

Daphne: You ask such huge questions, you two. The self is a difficult concept too, because it's not unitary. I talk about this in a book that Betsy [Warland] has edited called *InVersions*. That's where I've tried to talk about the self most clearly ("Changing the Focus"). The thing about memory is that there isn't one authoritative version, just as there isn't one self that would authorize that version. So it gets played out in different ways according to how you're approaching it. There's a lot of the unknown in the self, and memories are just those sparks that we salvage, and as soon as you catch a spark, it burns in a particular way, according to the context. I'm finding this really strongly in fiction actually, much more than in poetry where I'm not really concerned with the credibility of a memory. In fiction there's so much more of a character you have to anchor every thing to, but then the credibility of that character arises as she speaks. I don't feel such constraints in poetry. Now I'm interested in character, I don't want to dispense with character, because each character embodies a viewpoint, another version, and that tension between the different versions is what interests me. Simone de Beauvoir once wrote that as soon as you write a memory it begins to disappear, all you've got is the version written down in print, you can't remember what other versions there might be because the print version takes over. Which is a rather frightening concept because if you're writing about your life it means you're erasing memory as you reconstruct it. But I think we do that anyway even when we tell stories to other people. We retell anecdotes, constructing another version even in the telling. So in some sense memory as an original is unascertainable. You can never get back to it, and again I like playing with that. I like crossing the boundaries between so-called fact and unreliable memory, unorthodox memory, or illegitimate memory, or the memory that is just an invention.

three "why not be excessive"

A CONVERSATION WITH ERIN MOURÉ

Interviewed by Pauline Butling & Susan Rudy

ALSO KNOWN AS EIRIN MOURE, ERÍN MOURE, AND "ERIN MOURÉ," by publishing under several names, or what she calls "heteronyms" (McCance 9), Erin Mouré has "belie[d] the possibility of a strict identity" (Jarraway 73). In *Pillage Laud* (1999) she explains: "'Erin Mouré' is a biological product in the usual state of flux, containing organic and inorganic elements extending backward and forward in time, but tending as do all organisms toward homeostasis, in spite of entropic forces. Erin Mouré is an indicator of a social structure projected onto this organism" (99). *O Cidadán* (2002), her most recent book, "argues for a notion of frontier or border as a line that admits filtrations, that leaks…. Identity finds its stability in uncertainty, in the fluidity of limits, in the 'not yet'" (Mouré in McCance 2).

A poet, essayist, translator, freelance editor, communications specialist, and occasional teacher in Montréal, Mouré was born in 1955 and raised in Calgary, Alberta. After moving to Vancouver in 1974 she began writing poetry, finding encouragement initially from the Vancouver Industrial Writers Union. Her first book of poetry, *Empire, York Street* (1979), was nominated for a Governor

General's Award. In the suite of poems *The Whisky Vigil* (1981) she explains her early practice: "by uniting poems, exhortations, and addresses of varying objects," she writes, the suite "creates two characters unlike anyone alive, who have, nonetheless, lived like this: Although they break away from identification as individuals, they cannot break free of what is real."

In 1984, she moved to Montréal where she became involved with the Francophone feminist community through her then partner, writer Gail Scott. From that point on, her poetry became more overtly feminist as well as more formally innovative and socially conscious. With *Furious* (winner of the Governor General's Award for Poetry 1988), Mouré emerged as a major figure in the field of experimental, feminist poetry, a woman trying to *"move the force in language from the noun/verb centre. To de/centralize the force inside the utterance from the noun/verb, say, to the preposition. Even for a moment. To break the vertical hold"* (94) as she does in "Rolling Motion" (*Furious* 35): "your face in my neck & / arms dwelling upward face / in my soft leg open / lifted upward airborne soft / face into under into rolling / over every upward motion / rolling open over your /Face in my neck again over turning" (35).

In subsequent books, Mouré has extended her reputation for feminist formal innovation by making increasingly complex demands on her readers. *WSW* (*West South West*) (1989), for example, is a series of linked poems around the subject of "west" which are presented as versions or readings of one another: "The Beauty of Furs" appears alongside "The Beauty of Furs: A Site Glossary"; "order, or red ends" is followed by eight poems titled "order 2"–"order 9." *Sheepish Beauty, Civilian Love* (1993) explores "beauty" and "love" in lesbian and civic contexts: "As if dreams were a language that includes the social surface / of the body, 'signal fire' in the desert as the song says, the / body's lamp glowing, armpits & breasts & pectoral muscle. / Signifier. We see our selves moving. In the dream one's own / body signifies, at least. (But can we read it?)" ("Hope Stories" 102).

Mouré's selected poems *The Green Word* (1994) was followed by *Search Procedures*, a finalist for the Governor General's Award in 1996. In 1999, *A Frame of the Book* (or *The Frame of a Book*) was co-published by Anansi in Canada and Sun and Moon press in the U.S. *Pillage Laud: cauterizations, vocabularies, cantigas, topiary, prose* (1999) draws on the uncanny potential in software-generated prose to produce "lesbian sex poems" since, unlike speech, the freeware program "MacProse" is "incapable of generating a cliché because it has no culture and has never met anyone" (Mouré reading). In 2002 Mouré published *O Cidadán*, winner of the Governor General's Award for Poetry, her twelfth book and the last in the trilogy that began with *Search Procedures* (1996) and *A Frame of the Book* (1999). David Jarraway describes it as "often nothing short of breathtaking," "a densely theoretical disquisition on female subjectivity in the present day" (75) that Mouré describes as "a reading practice in a community of others" (*O Cidadán* 141).

Erin Mouré continues to live and work in Montréal. Indeed what she calls "Canadian translation"—"sited in our values and context" (Mouré in McCance 10)—has become "part of my poetic practice; the play between languages is very important to me, for it shows up the gaps in my own language and expression. Lets me make English go where it won't naturally go" (Mouré in McCance 7). *Sheep's Vigil by a Fervent Person* (nominated for the Griffin Poetry Prize for 2001) is what she calls a "Transelation" of Alberto Cairo / Fernando Pessoa's *O Guardador de Rebanhos*. In that book she managed to translate herself by signing the book Eirin Moure, the Portuguese spelling of her name. She has also translated the work of other poets, most notably Nicole Brossard. With Robert Majzels, she "translated lovingly" (Knutson 125) both *Installations* (1999) and *Museum of Bone and Water* (2003).

The poetry of Erin Mouré has been anthologized for more than twenty years: in Douglas Barbour and Marni Stanley's *Writing Right: New Poetry by Canadian Women* (1982), in three 1984 anthologies: Mary di Michele's *Anything is Possible* (1984), Ken Norris' *Canadian Poetry Now: 20 Poets of the 80's* (1990), *Women & Words: The Anthology/Les Femmes et les Mots: Une Anthologie*, and, Rosemary Sullivan's *Poetry by Canadian Women* (1989). More recently, her work is available in Gary Geddes' *20th Century Poetry and Poetics* (1996), Sharon Thesen's *The New Long Poem Anthology* (1991, 2001), Mary Margaret Sloan's *Moving Borders: Three Decades of Innovative Writing by Women* (1998), *Uncommon Wealth: An Anthology of Poetry in English* (ed. Besner et al. 1997), 15 *Canadian Poets x 3* (ed. Geddes 4th edition 2001), and *A New Anthology of Canadian Literature in English* (ed. Bennett and Brown 2002). See Dickson "'Signals across boundaries': non-congruence and Erin Mouré's 'Sheepish Beauty, Civilian Love'" (1997), Dopp "'Field of potentialities': reading Erin Mouré" (1999), Carrière *Writing in the feminine in French and English Canada* (2002), and Rudy "'what can atmosphere with / vocabularies delight?': Excessively Reading Erin Mouré" (2004).

—*SR*

three

Pauline Butling: We'd like to start by talking about the interview structure, what it assumes and how speaking within the context of an interview frames, or limits, the discussion. I noticed in your interview with Janice Williamson that you didn't really like being interviewed, that you didn't like questions that might solidify your public identity.

Erin Mouré: Yes. Like everyone, I don't like people trying to solidify me.

Susan Rudy: Yet isn't talking to each other a crucial aspect of community building?

Erin: I agree, totally. I believe that thinking is really contextual. It's an action and not a thing and you need context to go further. Talking to others helps create context.

Pauline: Speaking of context: what was the context for *Furious* (1988)? Your poetics seemed to shift dramatically with that book.

Erin: With *Furious* I didn't want to write another version of *Domestic Fuel* (1985). I was tired of doing what I was doing, dissatisfied with what I was calling the Mouré poem, and I didn't want to keep on doing that. It didn't interest me anymore. A lot of poets get to a point where they are just repeating themselves and never get out of it. I think a real catalyst or turning point for me was the Women & Words conference in 1983.

Susan: Did you have a feminist community before that?

Erin: No, not specifically a feminist writing community, though I did know women who were working on *Kinesis,* the community women's paper in Vancouver.

Pauline: Did you meet many writers at Women & Words?

Erin: I heard many writers, rather than meeting them. I was very much in the background. But it opened up my thinking about women and language. It opened my eyes, and once you have your eyes opened you start to see other things that had just drifted by you somehow. The next February I was in Montréal with some women who were trying to put together a Mont-réal branch of Women & Words. That was when the first issue of *Tessera* came out. I can remember opening it up, and feeling that every page was something I just had to read.

Pauline: Was that when you first met Gail Scott?

Erin: Actually, yes. So I read that first issue and started reading the books and articles that had been mentioned by writers in that first issue, using it as a kind of template for my own reading. I started to read Kristeva, Irigaray, and Dale Spender's *Man Made Language.* And I listened to and talked with Gail, who shared a lot with me. At that time I didn't speak or read French well enough to read literature. I had just started to read the front page of the newspaper. Any access to French was through Gail, apart from what I'd encountered at Women & Words in translation. And Gail questioned many of my attitudes. I didn't come from a community where you talked about writing itself. Everybody was writing, but nobody talked about it in terms of feminism, or in terms of the workings of language. The only context I had found where people talked about writing was the Vancouver Industrial Writers Union, which was full of problems for me.

Pauline: Who belonged to that group when you were involved with it?

Erin: Tom Wayman, Phil Hall, Kirsten Emmett and Zoë Landale. At least those people talked a little about writing, and I worked with Phil Hall and the others to organize a reading series. Yet the whole orientation of work poetry and the theory about it all really was problematic for me. It was populist in a way that seemed to negate things I wanted to explore.

Pauline: Were you reading any women writers then? Daphne Marlatt, Phyllis Webb, Dorothy Livesay?

Erin: I'd read Daphne's *Steveston*, all of Margaret Atwood, but that was more in the mid-seventies, when I was going to university. I'd read Phyllis Webb, and Dorothy Livesay as well. I also read a lot of [George] Bowering. I go through phases of Bowering. I always liked Bowering.

Susan: Did you like American feminist poets?

Erin: I had a hard time with what I found in that era by American feminist poets. I tried to read Adrienne Rich and Marge Piercy. During this time in Vancouver I was dissatisfied with my own work, and I was getting different ideas, and was looking and looking. But reading Rich and Piercy profoundly dissatisfied me. I thought, well, if this is what you have to do to write feminist poetry, then I'm not sure I'm going to enjoy it. One of my favourite writers when I was in Vancouver in the '70s was Jack Spicer. I had *The Collected Books of Jack Spicer* [1975], the one with the Blaser essay ["The Practice of Outside"]. Susan Penner, Dennis Wheeler's partner, lent it to me and then I bought it. It's a book I read over and over. It's still on my shelf of critical books.

Susan: What did you like in his poetry?

Erin: I liked his sense of humour and the way his phrases played off things. His writing, to me, proceeded like thought itself. It was insistent, wry, rich, but not flat narration. It played with elements of flat narration, but in a different way. Most of the other American poets I read in that era were men like Philip Levine and W.S. Merwin and James Wright, who I still quite like, and Frank O'Hara.

Pauline: What about canonical writers, the overcoat of dead poets?

Erin: I don't have a very good background in the dead poets.

Pauline: Did you study literature at university?

Erin: I didn't go to university long enough to study anything. I studied philosophy actually. I figured I would read literature by myself, but philosophy—like formal logic, epistemology, and metaphysics—I figured I wouldn't just bring it to the beach and read it so I'd better take courses.

Susan: In your poetry you use a particular discourse that includes words like "civilian" and "polis"? Where does that come from?

Erin: I think a lot about civic responsibility and the place of a person in a community. I'm also wondering how responsibility and community fit together, especially for me, being a feminist, a lesbian and a woman. How can you be responsible to another person when you have a hard enough time being yourself? How is a person who they are? You're not the same in isolation; your relations in community form you as an individual.

Pauline: Does feminist analysis help you to understand this?

Erin: I think feminist analysis gives a different way of looking at the problem and a different way of looking at your place in it. Things are not very nice out there especially if you're poor or if you lack resources, if you don't have a job, or if your voice is not linked to power. And I see a system that works to lull people so that they don't think. Everything is commodified and every form of protest gets reabsorbed. That's the way the system continues. So I look at the system structurally, look at it as process. Sometimes it's enough to make you ask, "Can I cancel out of this planet?" And that question makes me wonder what makes people go on. One thing I was trying to do in *Sheepish Beauty, Civilian Love* was to ask "Why does hope exist? What is it?" Maybe in the long run this was why I got into writing poetry instead of finishing a degree in philosophy. The question "Why does hope exist?" wouldn't be interesting to philosophers because hope is too tied into feelings.

Pauline: Yes, it's not rational enough. What about *Furious*? It seems quite philosophical.

Erin: With *Furious*, Gail and the space she had helped open up for me were really important. I guess I was ready to receive that space and ready to do something with it. She used to ask me why I acted as if thinking and writing were separate. I didn't realize that of course I was thinking about poems. Again, it's about conversation; if you lack a context, you can't sit there and talk, even if there are other people there, if nobody's giving back. You need somebody to challenge your preconceptions and challenge your paradigm. You can't challenge your own perceptions. Gail was important to me in that way. I started writing down what I was thinking when I was writing some of the poems, how I was trying to think out the poem.

Pauline: In *Furious* and even more so in *Search Procedures* your writing practices connect very specifically to feminist issues of speaking the lesbian subject and creating feminist subjectivity. To what extent are you consciously connecting feminist issues and language issues as you're writing?

Erin: Well, I am consciously working through and into women's relationship in and to language. I think I approach language with a feminist consciousness, consciousness of the history of women, how women are sited. When I was writing "Three Versions" I asked Gail, which one do you like? She read them and got really impatient with my question, asking, "Why do you have to choose a definitive version?" That phrase of hers has echoed in my head since then. I think it's become woven into my practice over the years.

Susan: So material that was previously footnoted became part of the text?

Erin: Yes. Instead of having "The Acts" separate from the poems, as in *Furious,* I now tend to bring thinking into the poem and make it interrogate the poem at the same time.

Pauline: You often bring different discourses and different subjects into the poem. But do you think using multiple discourses goes against the notion of empowering a feminist subjectivity?

Erin: I think at some point you realize that the subject is a construction, that you can construct it differently. Through perception, we construct reality. For most people the construction of reality—the selection that has to take place for "reality" to be seen—is already done before conscious thinking begins. Take vision as an example. When the impulses reach the retina, the visual cortex is doing constant comparing to try to define what you're seeing. When you first see something, especially out of the corner of your eye where things seem to move faster than they actually do, you sometimes have a sense that there's something there, and when you turn your head, there's nothing. Your brain was actually constructing, trying to compare things, to recognize from bits of information (for there are fewer rods and cones at the peripheries of sight) what you are seeing. It makes temporary mistakes that straight on vision corrects easily. Really, your brain is comparing visual material all the time, as long as you keep moving your eyes. Thinking about perception has really been interesting. We're beings whose brains are constantly making selections, comparisons, and rejections. We're always trying different little sort-orders and once we get a sort-order, a lot of information received later on just doesn't register. I like trying to use some of that 'extra' information in my writing. Why not use it instead of just rejecting it?

Susan: But it's not as though women don't exist, or that other ways of being-in-the-world don't exist. It's that the given sort-order mechanism can't see them. Is that why you want to have a different way of talking, because all that other stuff doesn't get sorted and ordered?

Erin: Well that's why a person needs conversation. When you talk you talk in all kinds of order. It's more interactive. Trying some of these levels of thinking or relating right on the page is interesting too. The possibilities of the page are far from exhausted!

Susan: What have you been reading about the brain? Are there a couple of books you could recommend on perception?

Erin: There's a book by Israel Rosenfield called *The Invention of Memory*. Here's some of what Rosenfield writes: "In determining the shape it is signals across the boundaries of structures that count." I think that's so incredible. It isn't the boundaries of structures that determine the shape; it's signals across the boundaries of structures. "How they are perceived to the human eye depends on how they are categorized, how they are organized in terms of other stimuli, not on their absolute structure." There are no absolute structures. There are other books too, such as Gerald Edelman's *The Remembered Present*. It's so interesting, looking at how the brain works, how we construct subjectivity, how community is structured and how you can break out of it.

Susan: Sheepish Beauty, Civilian Love begins with two quotations that speak directly to these subjects.

Erin: There's a lot of sadness in *Sheepish Beauty, Civilian Love.* "Je n'ai jamais entendu ma mère prononcer le mot bonheur" is jarring (epigraph). It rings true for me too, as if life's an unending struggle. I'd translate the whole quote as:

There's another world, I'm sure of it. My inner voice, especially that of my mother that I hear, affirms this. This troubles me, though, because that voice of my mother seems charged with contradiction. I never heard my mother say the word happiness. I think it has to do with that, with an indefinable happiness, a search for it born out of present unhappiness.

Susan: So, it's not just your own mother, but how the past has been for women?

Erin: Well, I think it says something about women's experience, which is still very true. Women are still subject to violence. We want to think that all this was an experience of our mothers or something. Women still don't leave battering men because they construct a reality in which they're fine, they're okay, they can deal with it.

Pauline: While we're on the subject of quotes, why do you quote Lorca, "¡Oh, cómo el trigo es tierno! ["O how the wheat is tender"] in the acknowledgements?

Susan: And in "Visible Spectrum"?

> "& all grain is Lorcan grain."
> All grain is the wheaten field with its jagged seam of
> red poppy,
> by which we recognize visibly the cry of the other.
> All wheat is tender.
> All wheat is this tender.
> All grain has listened to the heartbeat of birds
> & bowed down its stems, winded.
> (*Sheepish Beauty* 38)

Erin: It's a beacon, present as a light. It's not something commented upon in a conventional poetic way.

Pauline: Sheepish Beauty, Civilian Love is divided into several sections. Would you talk about how you shaped the book?

Erin: Before *Furious* I really just wrote poems one at a time, not necessarily related to one another. Then while writing "The Acts" in *Furious,* I got a sense of writing into the book because the poems started to affect each other. Since then I've had more of a sense of writing into a book, even if it's at first a really vague idea. There were originally only four sections in *Sheepish*

Beauty, Civilian Love. As well, I sometimes write things that don't fit into any of the sections and some that don't fit into the book. "Executive Suite" and "The Curious" (*Sheepish Beauty*) were written at the same time, long before *Sheepish Beauty*, but they didn't fit into *West South West*, which I was writing at the time, so I took them out. Sometimes there are notions that I want to work with, like the Lorcan grain, like coming from west-southwest of somewhere, and just thinking about how a person internalizes a landscape. How the wheat growing had something to do with growing up. It made me think about tenderness, thinking about the growth of grains. Then there's "The Vowel O" section. I always wished they had a vacation package to the vowel O. I wanted to live on the letter O. I thought it would be very relaxing to go to the letter O. And I knew I wanted to write a section of civic poems. I wanted *Sheepish Beauty, Civilian Love* to be more open to the exterior than *West South West* was.

Pauline: What do you mean by civic poems?

Erin: I was writing into the civic and the personal and how they are related. The working title of the book was "Seams": seams and notions of civic space seem to go together. The whole idea of the seam interests me because it's an edge, but it's not at the edge of anything. It's an end, but it's not. It's a place where material is folded over on itself. It's like an edge where you make the middle of something out of an edge. At times even in these poems, there's a seam or margin in the middle, as in "Everything." I actually wrote it across the page, in a sense across the reader's tendency to read it as two columns, one after the other.

> She saw everything there was to see. A part of her knew this,
> She took it into her mouth & saw it, & tried.
> the folded softness. The plans they made were of idiotic
> Arabic music played in the restaurant proportions, why not, they were
> (she was not *in* the restaurant). all impossible at the first level,
> (*Sheepish Beauty* 30)

If you read it across it seems all jumbled until you get to the end, and then it crosses over.

Pauline: You're obviously working with visual space, with "seams" on the page.

Erin: Yes. With perception too. Because no matter how much you try to read one way, your eye tries to read it the other. If you're reading down one column, your eye still looks to the side to see what's going on there. You read out of order, though you try to stop yourself. Even if you train yourself not to look across to the other side of the page, you see the whole page.

Susan: So your work requires alternative ways of reading. But few of us have learned how to read carefully and attentively at all, much less in relation to such complex texts.

Erin: Again, perception is about absorbing only what you're attentive to. And most people are only attentive to the expected. If you're attentive to the unexpected, you're constantly being proven wrong in your suppositions. Most people aren't used to that. They have a hard enough time being in the world without constantly paying attention to things that prove you wrong.

Susan: Especially women.

Erin: Yes. But it's important for me to explore these things and not be condescending to readers. I want readers to come to the work and get what they can. If they miss things, then those things are not important for them. I want people to realize that it doesn't have to mean one fixed thing all the time. New readings make new attentional elements visible or audible. You can also just get pleasure out of reading the words and revelling in the play and echo of meanings. In "photon scanner (blue spruce)," for example, the compositional page is the entire visible reading surface; that is, both sides of what we conventionally consider to be two pages (*Sheepish Beauty* 84–85).

Pauline: Yes, the meanings echo between the two pages? How do you read this aloud? Do you read across both pages?

Erin: No, I read the left page, then the right when I read it aloud. But the poem takes place differently when it's read silently. While you're reading the left side, you are conscious of the right side in your peripheral vision. The really short, single lines on the right side pull your attention to them, partly because the left-side sections are so dense on the page, the right side just looks easier. You start to read the right side, even while thinking you're not. You're not even reading all of the lines at that moment, or in the right order, but they're interesting little phrases. They seem quirky but also very directed. The space they make on the page interests you, even though you "should" be concentrating on reading the sections on the left side! The whole poem plays as well with the notion of left and right brain working together, and how it's the right brain that wants to organize global space, and the left that's full of the details, organizing the details.

Pauline: All the poems in this sequence follow the same format, of short, double-spaced lines on the right-hand page and longer, single-spaced lines on the left. And in the penultimate poem of the sequence, you write: "Eventually all poems fall into their seam or *gutter*" and "the voice (stutter) speech is reconstructed in the split across / two hemispheres" (*Sheepish Beauty* 92). You seem drawn to the excess and the noise at the seams of consciousness, as you write in the last stanza:

> What is in excess of the body pissed out or
> cut by the pages here, whose binding you must efface
> o reader to engage
> the hemispheres' simultaneous noise, this *consciousness*
> where thought & the body Are one
> (*Sheepish Beauty* 92)

Erin: I'm saying "the hemispheres' simultaneous noise" is consciousness. The way the body works governs how consciousness can occur. If we were embodied differently, if we had one eye in the side of our heads, we'd read this poem differently.

Susan: If we believe that things are straightforward, we'll stop before engaging with a text like this. Do you have to learn to be self-questioning before you can even start to read a poem like this?

Erin: People do have habits of reading that disrupt the surface of the writing. You read a bit here and you read a bit there when you read the newspaper. And you don't feel bad about it at all, you don't feel guilty. You just have to bring the same kind of reading skill to poems. You only learn one kind of reading in school, how to read something like *The Globe and Mail*. And it's important that they cover up other ways of reading, for all your life that one way will be used to sell you things. Nobody wants you to believe you can read in any other way, because getting pleasure from reading is not useful to commerce. You don't need anyone to sell you anything anymore, which is too dangerous to contemplate!

Pauline: I notice you use the prose poem a lot towards the end of *Sheepish Beauty*. What's the difference between your prose poems and the other poems?

Erin: I did a bunch of things with the prose poem for a while. To me it was interesting because I still had line breaks, line endings.

Pauline: So you wouldn't want them to be typeset as prose?

Erin: Well no, they were set as prose, but when the typesetting causes the lines to break in the wrong place, I've rewritten the lines. Words, sounds and parts of speech still have a certain weight. If they end up in the wrong place that changes the weight. When things didn't fit quite right I would rewrite part of the poem so it would fit in the space in the way I wanted it to, even though it looks like prose and the line breaks could be random. Actually, in this long poem, "Hope Stories" (*Sheepish Beauty* 102), there are three different shapes: there's one that's typically lyric, there's a narrow prose form that's a jagged right margin, and then there's a wide prose form that goes across the page, justified right. The three forms are ways of representing different kinds of thinking, just like in real life, where we have this poetic sense that registers and makes little disconnected stories about what's around us all the time. Nobody pays any attention to it normally. To have a conversation you have to suppress it. But if not you'll be off on all kinds of considerations and mullings that out loud might be considered tangential. Yet they are thought's trails, they shimmer, they're important.

Susan: Why do you sometimes put titles in quotation marks?

Erin: It creates a particular kind of attention.

Susan: But couldn't it mean "Don't take this seriously?" Is it an ironic gesture?

Erin: Perhaps I don't want people to take the title seriously. Or perhaps, as with a foreign word, it's in quotes so that people know to read past it, just read past it, but don't worry if it doesn't fit. Or perhaps it's admitting that it's not true, that what follows are "stories." So it's as if three kinds of thinking are going on simultaneously.

Pauline: Would you talk about the Christian frame of reference woven throughout your work, particularly the proposition of transubstantiation which I assume refers to language.

Erin: I'm a highly religious poet!

Pauline: I find your proposition of transubstantiation really interesting. Not just the notion of turning language into something that has body and blood, giving it that kind of substance. But also the process of taking a concept that is sacred and then desacralizing it, and making it work in a completely different way.

Erin: I guess that comes from my interest in structures or how things work. What's always interested me about Catholic dogma is that just saying something can make it true. And other people can say well no it's not true, but it actually is, because they said so, and that's it. It's an extreme example of constructing a reality.

Pauline: Were you raised Catholic?

Erin: Yes.

Pauline: Does colloquial language re-invest language with life or vitality? Is that one way to bring the word to life?

Erin: Well the way people say things has meaning, as in Wittgenstein, who is evoked in "The Notification of Birches." Use or use-value is in the saying. Mostly people just use phrases or words to get from one point to another in what they are saying, and they never think about this bridge they're building between what they say, and what is. It's the signals across the boundaries of structures that count. I'd rather focus on the signals that cross the boundaries.

Pauline: Is that what a synapse is? I'm thinking of the poems called "These Synapses" at the end of the book (*Sheepish Beauty* 128–33). Are synapses the "signals that cross boundaries"?

Erin: The synapse is the space between, the space that has to be jumped. When trying to articulate a feeling or state of mind, you can come at it from numerous angles and then you have to jump, and part of the structure is in making the jumps. An act. I talk about synapse at one point. Here it is, in "Fit":

> Synaptic channel to the chest, thru the shoulder.
> Synaptic pipeline to the lung, thru the shoulder.
> The shoulder joint the hand's link

to *the corridor of the body*,
the ball-joint &
myelitic coatings,
rounded bone,
the fit of one bone into another. Transmission from the fingers' whorls.
The chalky hands reaching down for the bar.
Legs braced.
The fit of it. The gloves & wrapped wrists.
The fit of some bones.

The chalky hands
ready to reach down to the weight
& lift it (clean) to the shoulders:
105 pounds.
("Fit" *Sheepish Beauty* 130)

This is actually talking about weightlifting. You put chalk on your hands, reach down for the bar, legs braced. You think you can't lift the weight and then, bang, you can. It's like getting everything to fit and then you can move.

Pauline: The first two poems in "These Synapses" are obviously love poems. How do they relate to the question of synapse?

Erin: It's like—when you touch somebody—how does that reach the centre of you. This has to do with synapses. There are these little narrative moments and it's a jump to get between them. The actual little events don't actually even have to do with the same people. They're not transcriptions of reality. And some of them are completely invented. It's dealing with being able to jump. Where does language bring you when you jump?

Pauline: The love poem has traditionally been *self*-expressive, but yours speak of desire and attraction without focussing on the self.

Erin: That's what I was aiming for. Just when it seems as if you are, it jumps, it goes somewhere else. It's just letting language take you. Your lexicon provokes you to think about other things because lexicons are so deep and zig-zaggy.

Pauline: Is this a process of association?

Erin: Oh definitely, although just calling it a process of association sounds kind of chintzy, but the lexicon, the word, is rich with association. The synapse is jumping to something new. When you learn something new, it's hard because you have to create new synapses. Otherwise you use the old ones. When a path is used more often, the little hairy endings of the nerves (the dendrite) grow. There's more hairy dendrite. So the synapses are shorter. When people try to solve a problem, when the old solution doesn't work, the problem goes around and around in the head and it refuses to make a new synaptic connection, so you get frustrated. A lot of people can't stand that frustration so instead of letting the thing go around the circuit and find a new solution, they change the problem so the old solution fits. You see people doing that a lot in their lives.

Pauline: They do it in poetry all the time too.

Erin: The synapse is not always ballet leaps across the page. It's often very subtle things. The synapse is in the nerve structure.

Pauline: I remember Charles Olson saying that the synapse is easy, it's the neural condition that's the challenge. It's what you do before that makes the leap possible.

Erin: Gerald Edelman and other people of the late 70s did a lot of research on neurons, which is now an accepted part of neurology. They show how the whole neural process works. What Olson says makes sense, because you have these conditioned nerves that you have to get away from. It's easier to keep going the same way. If you're writing poetry, you can't go one way all the time. You have to get off the track. You have jumps to make. Or you keep writing the same old poem, the "cultural poem." I was trying to reproduce in the form of the poem a synaptic experience by having these jumps between sections. Our range of experience, the way our minds and bodies work, is so much richer than the cultural poem.

Susan: Are you going to start producing work in digital form? Come to think of it, why are you writing on the page anyway?

Erin: Well the page is more interesting than we realize. The page will not die, we can still do more things with it.

Susan: Your writing strategies already make readers aware of their bodies and the body's relation to the page. Your pages discourage a split between mind and body, and somehow bring them together.

Erin: But the response I get sometimes is that this requires theory to understand, and people shy away from theory. I always tell people that theory is just thinking, that you're thinking too. And this thinking of yours right now is your theory. We're all thinking all the time. If you don't think about thinking, the monoculture functions. If we could get a critical mass then we could do it, we could think ourselves somewhere else entirely, but forget it. You'd have a better chance of taking off in a spaceship.

Pauline: Fortunately, there are still writers who believe that it's important to think about thinking.

Erin: It's not worth living otherwise. There are nice times—just seeing lilacs, for example, will do as a justification for human existence—but it doesn't hold for most of the year.

four **Struggle**
and Community,
Possibility and Poetry

Interviewed by Pauline Butling

Dionne Brand is a poet, novelist, and essayist living in Toronto. Her eight volumes of poetry include *Land to Light On* (1997), which won both the Governor General's Award for Poetry and the Trillium Award for Literature, and *thirsty* (2003), which won the Pat Lowther Award for Poetry and was nominated for the Trillium Award and the Griffin Poetry Prize. Born in 1953 in Guayguayare, Trinidad, Brand immigrated to Toronto at the age of seventeen where she became immersed in the Black and feminist liberation movements of the 1970s. She completed a B.A. in English and Philosophy at the University of Toronto in 1975 and an M.A. in History and Philosophy at the Ontario Institute for Studies in Education in 1989.

Throughout the 1970s and 1980s, she also worked as a cultural critic and community worker for various organizations, such as the Black Education Project, The Immigrant Women's Health Centre, The Black Women's Collective, and the Caribbean People's Development Agency. She edited and/or wrote articles for many activist publications, including *Spear, Fuse, Network, Our Lives,*

The Harriet Tubman Review, Fireweed, and *Resources for Feminist Research.* Brand's non-fiction includes a collection of oral histories about the struggles of people of colour in Toronto—*Rivers Have Sources, Trees Have Roots: Speaking of Racism* (with Krisantha Sri Bhaggiyadatta 1986)—and a history of Black women: *No Burden to Carry: Narratives of Black Working Women in Ontario, 1920's–1950* (1991). In 1994, she published *Bread Out Of Stone,* a book of essays for which Adrienne Rich called her "a cultural critic of uncompromising courage, an artist in language and ideas, an intellectual conscience for her country" (back cover). Her most recent non-fiction publication, *A Map to the Door of No Return* (2001), is a meditation on Blackness in the diaspora.

Reflecting her marxist and feminist thinking, Brand's poetry, essays, and fiction explore issues of diasporic dislocation, restrictive gender and race categories, and colonial oppressions. Her poetry career began with five books in quick succession: *'Fore Day Morning* (1978); *Earth Magic* (poetry for children 1979); *Primitive Offensive* (1982); and *Winter Epigrams & Epigrams to Ernesto Cardenal in Defense of Claudia* (1983), a book of pithy and often witty epigrammatic poems about surviving Toronto's interminable winters together with a "Defense of Claudia," a feminist rewriting of the traditional betrayal story. The final book in this cluster, *Chronicles of the Hostile Sun* (1984), is Brand's lyric response to the invasion by the United States of Grenada, which occurred while she was working there as an information Officer for the Caribbean People's Development Agency.

In Brand's first five books, the style is fairly traditional, with modernist-style, sparse images and short lines. *No Language is Neutral* (1990) marks a significant shift in her poetry. Formally, she experiments with prose poems, longer lines, and demotic speech; thematically, she begins to articulate her newly-discovered lesbian sexuality, especially in the opening and closing sections, appropriately titled "hard against the soul": "This / grace, you see, come as a surprise and nothing till now knock on my teeming skull, then, these warm / watery syllables, a woman's tongue so like a culture, / plunging toward stones not yet formed into flesh" (36). She also continues to articulate diasporic dislocations: "Our / singing parched, drying in the silence after the / chicken and ham and sweet bread effort to taste like / home…. // Well, even / our nostalgia was a lie, skittish as the truth these / bundle of years" (30) and to delve into personal history in the section titled "Return"—poems based on childhood memories—and in the section titled "No Language is Neutral," a prose poem sequence that articulates the "grammar" of oppression: "a morphology of rolling chain and copper gong," and "language seared in the spine's unravelling" (23). Overall the book testifies to the power of poetry to reshape identity by reworking language constructs. In *Land to Light On* (1997), Brand continues her experiments with poetic form. The book consists of numbered sequences of mostly prose poems, loosely organized around seven provocative section titles, such as "I have been losing roads," "All that has happened since," "Land to light on," and "Dialectics." Mostly written while living in Burnt River (in rural Ontario), Brand writes of her own and others' outsider experiences in hostile cultural and physical landscapes: "If I am peaceful in this discomfort, is not peace, / is getting used to harm" (3). In a review of *Land to Light On*, Judith Fitzgerald writes: "Every once in a rare while a book of poetry—because it is poetry—appears on the literary landscape and breaks your heart.... The impeccably crafted sequence contains the spirit and soul of human fealty, which acts as a shield against the brutality of human history" (*Globe & Mail* D11). Brand's next poetry book, *thirsty* (2002), is a sociopolitical narrative of life in Toronto. Taking her cue from the story of a dying man's last word, "thirsty" (the man is shot by police while working in his garden), Brand ponders Toronto's spiritually parched environment, its continual marginalization of the poor, and, paradoxically, its beauty. She writes passionately (and compassionately) of its people and places: "This city is beauty / unbreakable and amorous as eyelids" (1); "In the kitchen her tongue parts the flesh of avocados / and akees, / the stiff tough saltiness of dried cod; the waves of chatter / are light" (43); and "Spring darkness is forgiving. It doesn't descend / abruptly before you have finished work, / it approaches palely waiting for you / to get outside to witness another illumined hour" (57).

Brand's fiction includes the acclaimed novel *In Another Place, Not Here*—a 1998 New York Times notable book—and *Sans Souci and Other Stories* (1988). Her most recent novel, *At the Full & Change Of The Moon* (1999), spans six generations, two wars and the violence of the late twentieth century. *The Village Voice* included her in their 1999 *Writers on the Verge Literary supplement* and it was a *Los Angeles Times* Notable Book of the Year, 1999. Brand has produced four documentary films: *Older, stronger, wiser* (1989), *Long time comin'* (1991), *Sisters in the Struggle* (1991), and *Listening for Something: Adrienne Rich and Dionne Brand in Conversation* (1996).

Brand has served as Writer-in-residence at the Halifax City Regional Library in 1980, the University of Toronto (1990–91), and The University of Guelph (2003–04). She was an Assistant Professor of English at the University of Guelph (1992–94), held the Ruth Wynn Woodward Chair in Women's Studies at Simon Fraser University in Vancouver (2001–02) and, after a semester as Distinguished Professor at St Lawrence University in Canton NY, returned to the University of Guelph in 2004 as Professor and University Research Chair.

Her prose, essays, and fiction have been widely published in magazines. Her work also appears in numerous anthologies, including *The New Long Poem Anthology* (ed. Thesen 1991, 2001), *Grammar of Dissent: Poetry and Prose* (ed. Morrell 1994), *Fiery Spirits: Canadian Writers of African Descent* (ed. Black 1995), *Making a Difference: Canadian Multicultural Literature* (ed. Kamboureli 1996), *Uncommon Wealth: An Anthology of Poetry in English* (ed. Besner et al. 1997), *15 Canadian Poets x 3* (ed. Geddes 4th edition 2001), and *A New Anthology of Canadian Literature in English* (eds. Bennett and Brown 2002). Critical discussions of Brand's poetry include Erin Mouré, "A Love that Persists"; Meira Cook, "Partisan body: performance and the female body in Dionne Brand's *No Language Is Neutral*"; Lynette Hunter; "After Modernism: Alternative Voices in the Writings of Dionne Brand, Claire Harris, and Marlene Philip"; and Jason Wiens, "'Language seemed to split in two': national ambivalence (s) and Dionne Brand's 'no language is neutral.'"

—*PB*

four

Pauline Butling: Why did you start writing and what contexts or communities were supportive or generative for you?

Dionne Brand: After I talked to you this morning about that question, I thought of Naipaul's new book, *A Way in the World.* Finally, Naipaul addresses and responds to the texts that constructed him in Trinidad in the 1930s, 1940s, and 1950s, the same texts that constructed me, the anti-colonial texts created in the Caribbean.

Pauline: Does he name them?

Dionne: He doesn't. I recognize them because I come from the same place. I think that he is responding to Eric Williams' *Capitalism and Slavery,* to C.L.R. James' *Black Jacobins* and *Minty Alley,* and to the language of anti-colonialism he would have encountered in those texts as a young man.

Pauline: Did you read all those texts?

Dionne: Yes, we all did. And the anti-colonial struggle came in so many ways there, with major strikes of plantation workers or oil field workers on all those islands.

Pauline: And this happened in the 1950s, 1960s?

Dionne: Yes, along with an early form of Black Nationalism, an anti-colonial Black Nationalism that much of that leadership represented, however poorly and badly they turned out.

Pauline: So the momentum started after the Second World War?

Dionne: Yes, independence, pro-independence movements and so on. Those were the texts that I read growing up. As much as I had to read Wordsworth or Shakespeare and all of that in school, I also read those texts.

Pauline: In school or outside of school?

Dionne: Outside of school. And here I'm using texts in a larger sense, not just books but...

Pauline: The cultural scripts? You were born at a time of competing cultural scripts?

Dionne: Yes, in 1953, luckily. So I turned out to have, not the slavishness, if you will, of a Naipaul for British culture. Instead I could critique it even as I learned it, even as it has probably scripted my aesthetics in some way. I had the pro-independence movement, which has appealed to me since I was a kid. I didn't want to hang on to British culture, but for Naipaul's generation as well as Walcott's, there was much more of a pull to agree with its colonial premises.

Pauline: They had been really seduced by it, hadn't they.

Dionne: Even as I say that, though, I know people of the same generation who were not seduced by it, like Martin Carter from Guyana or like Kamau Braithwaite or George Lamming. There were political differences among people of the same generation.

Pauline: So you had very different influences?

Dionne: Yes, and therefore I had choice. And I chose the position that would allow me integrity, a future, and a vision. Because if I had believed what Naipaul believed, I would have had to believe that I was incredibly flawed as a human being, deeply flawed, down to the texture of my skin. So the texts from this rising anti-colonial movement were what I read. If the anti-colonial movement began to reveal the possibilities for being a Black person in the world, then the 1960s and the Black Power movement in the States, for me at any rate, and the Civil Rights movement, solidified my sense of those possibilities. Also, the African liberation struggles in Mozambique, Angola, Zimbabwe. C.L.R. James had hooked up with George Padmore and with Kwame Nkrumah from Ghana to form the Pan-African movement earlier in the 1950s also.

Pauline: Who was George Padmore?

Dionne: He was Trinidadian. Other Caribbean intellectuals, Black nationalist intellectuals or Communist intellectuals like C.L.R. James got together and formed the Pan-African movement with Kwame Nkrumah and others. Suddenly, what you could call a Black world, or a Black consciousness, came together for me. When I got to Toronto, there were many organizations: local struggles, like the Black students' movement on the campus at the University of Toronto which advocated a pre-university program for disadvantaged people who would be Black or Native or poor white, a transitional program.

Pauline: Were you involved in that?

Dionne: Peripherally, just as part of the Black Students' Union. Those Black Students' Unions were—on every campus—the core of support for the African liberation movements, as well as community organizations. Community organizations were beginning the fight against racism in the school system, the educational system in Toronto and so on, before there were things like race relations anywhere. That was 1972, 1973. I worked at a place called the Black Education Project. And I was part of African liberation support committees. The work was local, whether it was against racism in the police force, police brutality, or in the education system, and then it was also international work, in support of African liberation struggles and the American civil rights movements in the States.

Pauline: That must have been really exciting.

Dionne: Oh, was it ever. I remember around 1973 or 1975 an enormous Black people's conference was held at the Harbour Collegiate in Toronto. Amiri Baraka came. I remember the magnificence of that moment in the auditorium of the Harbour Collegiate, the singing and the assuredness of it. It was so lovely to be young then and have support for your integrity and verification of your existence.

Pauline: Were a lot of writers involved? Did you have much contact with writers in that period?

Dionne: Well I went to work to learn journalism. But I didn't even call it that then. It was just struggle work that you did. And the struggle also needed poets, it needed preachers and poets.

Pauline: And you got named as a person who could be part of that?

Dionne: No, I just went in there. But everybody had a function. As a matter of fact, what had influenced me more than ever was the sound of people like Sonia Sanchez, Nikki Giovanni, Don Leome and Amiri Baraka, the Black poets of the 60s, and what they were saying and how they were saying it. And a whole bunch of us tried to form a parallel set of poets and writers in Toronto. So I went to work at *Spear* magazine. And when I say work, I really don't mean work for money, I mean struggle work. At *Spear* this very interesting fellow named J. Ashton Brathwaite encouraged me. He later changed his name to Odimumba Kwamdela. He had been a soldier in the British army, and had actually written a book called *Black British Soldier*. And he had also written another book called *Niggers... This is Canada*. He was very generous with young people, taught us how to lay out a magazine, and encouraged us to speak and to write poetry. I had decided much earlier that I was going to be a writer and I thought this was a good place to begin. There was lots of encouragement to write.

Pauline: Was *Spear* a literary magazine?

Dionne: No, it was a general magazine, but it had a good component of poetry and short stories in it.

Pauline: I remember *The Georgia Straight* in Vancouver had a literary supplement for a while too. A lot of the lefty magazines or struggle magazines included poetry.

Dionne: Because poetry was also supposed to be put to the defense of the struggle, because you were supposed to be able to appeal to people through the feeling art produces, not just on a mechanical level, but also...

Pauline: On an emotional level?

Dionne: Yes, so that's what I did. I began to write and, with encouragement, became more daring about reading in public, at community events.

Pauline: Were there other writers in the community?

Dionne: Well, yes. Makeda Silvera worked on another paper called *Contrast*. And there were lots of other aspiring writers. At that time, everyone thought they could write a poem.

Pauline: Ayanna Black wasn't around then, was she?

Dionne: She was around but she didn't come and do the paper thing. She was a little older than we were. She had been a nurse. Who else? Clifton Joseph, Lillian Allen, Roger McTair, and Marlene Nourbese Philip were around. Not around the paper, but just in the community and doing things.

Pauline: Would you meet at places where people gave readings? What context brought people together?

Dionne: Community events. Some community organizations, like the one I worked for, the Black Education Project, would have a cultural day. There were also cultural evenings. If someone came to make a speech, we would also hear a poet, a singer, a dancer and a drummer. So there would always be a cultural aspect to the evenings where we read whatever we had been working on.

Pauline: So you had an immediate audience?

Dionne: Oh, totally.

Pauline: Did you feel that you had to write in a certain way for that audience?

Dionne: I was torn in those days. When I was seventeen or eighteen I felt I had to write like an African American poet. That kind of declamatory style. I started writing that way and then, at some point, I recognized that I couldn't sustain it because it wasn't my language. I needed to be much more aware of the twists and turns of the language that I was working in order to use it fully. So that declamatory style shaped the poetry in the beginning but then I drifted away from it.

Pauline: Were there people with whom you talked about writing? About how you might work with language?

Dionne: Yes. A number of us were from the Caribbean. We were immigrants, so we talked about whether we would write in the demotic or whether we would write in standard English, and what that would mean and so on.

Pauline: Was that discussion politicized in terms of how language colonizes?

Dionne: Definitely. But you had a lot of breadth even in the standard, in a formal kind of standard—god knows there are lots of standards—so you had choices even if you worked in standard as to how you would undermine that language. But there was also the pull of the demotic. And then if you use the demotic, what are you doing with it anyway? Are you truly plumbing it for the range of things that it can do or, within the context of a Canada or a Toronto, are you only plumbing it for recognition by your audience?

Pauline: For an identity?

Dionne: Or for laughter or for all of those things, including the need, for an immigrant audience, to hold things static, the way they were back home.

Pauline: Conservatism actually.

Dionne: Yes. Deep conservatism. The fundamentalism of leaving intact nostalgic comparisons. Saying "this wouldn't have been so there," "this wouldn't have been so 'back home'." When, in fact, we didn't even know how things were there anymore.

Pauline: You don't use the demotic much in your poetry do you? Just in your fiction?

Dionne: I use *a* demotic. I gave Claire [Harris] this book to read for me because I was having a little trepidation about editing it. And she said to me, "Look here, tell them that you use two demotics. You use a standard demotic and then you use a demotic that signifies the working class." And she was right. When I use the standard I don't use it in the standard way. I don't construct a sentence as a standard English speaker or writer does, because I don't even think there are "standard" English speakers. But at that time I just didn't like how I thought whites in Canada read the demotic and was not willing to write that way just to amuse anyone. I decided to use the demotic when I could examine it much more carefully. I wanted to work it like a language rather than work it as an example of culture. I didn't want to write in the demotic until I thought I had a hold of what I could really do in it. My first attempt, or maybe it was my second attempt, was "Blossom."

Pauline: In "Blossom" you use the demotic in her speech rhythms and vocabulary. In your poetry, it's more of a rhythmic structure. As you say at the back of *The New Long Poem Anthology*, you try, in *No Language Is Neutral*, "to make the poem sound like a constant and full humming"; that you "intended it to be felt as a sustained rhythm...using...what Henry Louis Gates calls 'Black rhetorical tropes'" (353). This is quite different from your use of it in "Blossom," where it's more a technique of characterization.

Dionne: Exactly. In a sense "Blossom" was my first attempt at formally practicing it, and seeing if I could do it, not just for its difference, but if I could integrate it into her entire life. And I think I was successful at that, but I still had a lot of work to do on it. In *No Language* I suddenly gave myself the wherewithal to speak in it and to just continue until, as the structure of my own language in my brain worked, it slipped into a kind of standard demotic. And then it slipped back out of that standard. And I think I followed the root of my language in my head. And I determined never to use it in *No Language* to any of the effects that it had been used before. That is to the effect of humour or to the effect of an easy allusion. But that it would be used to convey everything, the depth of feelings, the depth of tragedy or terror. You know, even as I say that, I don't know. I mean, of course colonialism is always at the root of these choices somehow.

Pauline: Yes, for sure.

Dionne: In *No Language*, I found a way to slip in and out of these two demotics with no compunction at all. It meant totally opening the language that I had learned and knew to its fullest potential. And so it suddenly wasn't jerky or different. And I also didn't care who understood it or not. I never do anyway. That's one thing I decided about audience a long time ago. That the audience would simply have to walk in if they could and if they couldn't, well, they could go read something else.

Pauline: Perhaps because you were reading at community centres with a Black audience, audience was not an issue. It wasn't necessarily a question of people understanding. There was a social thing going on.

Dionne: And even within that audience, I also had to resist only saying what was appealing. And I also had to resist giving that audience, which was mainly an immigrant Canadian audience, the salve of its rightness because it was an immigrant audience. So I had to, as Langston Hughes says, not simply represent but also break, violate.

Pauline: Otherwise you're just reinforcing colonialism. Would you read an example from *No Language Is Neutral*?

Dionne: In this piece, for example, I fall into the real demotic for a moment. Listen:

> Here is history too. A backbone bending and
> unbending without a word, heat, bellowing these
> lungs spongy, exhaled in humming, the ocean, a
> way out and not anything of beauty, tipping turquoise
> and scandalous. The malicious horizon made us the
> essential thinkers of technology. How to fly gravity,
> how to balance basket and prose reaching for
> murder. Silence done curse god and beauty here,
> people does hear things in this heliconia peace
> a morphology of rolling chain and copper gong
> now shape this twang, falsettos of whip and air
> rudiment this grammar. Take what I tell you. When
> these barracks held slaves between their stone
> halters, talking was left for night and hush was idiom
> and hot core. ("no language is neutral" *No Language Is Neutral* 23)

It just seemed to swing right into it. Maybe because the other demotic that I'm using at the beginning isn't the real demotic. You don't have to put the other in quotation marks, this demotic falls from it.

Pauline: You use it again in your novel *In Another Place, Not Here* in a different way?

Dionne: I hope so. Yes, I think so. For the most part many novels used British formal standard English writing. And used the demotic only in the dialogue. And so for me it felt like the dialogue just stuck out there. The dialogue demarcated the difference. And the difference that was being demarcated was a difference of class and race and all those things. And therefore it subjugated the characters in the book. And so I thought, how can I do it? The novel is called *In Another Place, Not Here* from a line in "no language" (34). I thought, what is the idiomatic field that would contain this, whether it be dialogue or monologue, whether it be first person narrative or dialogue. What idiomatic field shall I place it in for it to be comfortable in that space? So the novel's first forty or so pages are a first person narrative of this woman who is a cane cutter, so it's also about class. And she's talking about her life and a certain revelation in her life, and she's also talking about history. Her own philosophical discourse on life. Self-consciousness isn't given to working-class people in novels.

So how would I write this self-awareness, this self-consciousness, and this philosophical rumination?

Pauline: A kind of Tillie Olson "I Stand Here Ironing" position?

Dionne: Yes, a position that leaves her with the integrity of her thoughts and speech and everything. And also shows that she is a formidable speaker. People really think that somehow working class people are incapable of depth of thought, which is a complete lie. Quite the opposite. So I made the decision to start the novel with the first person narrative, so she establishes it as her novel in a way.

Pauline: You haven't framed her within another discourse that undermines her story.

Dionne: Right. That's precisely why I didn't begin the novel with the third person narrator, even though she is not the distant, omniscient, know-it-all narrator. She is also implicated in the narrative.

Pauline: She doesn't have a position from which to judge?

Dionne: Well, I'm sure she pulls for something or other. But it's not as a distant narrator. It's also an internal narrator, a further kind of internality to the first person narrations in the book.

Pauline: Can we return to the 1970s? Were you ever involved in *Fireweed* or other literary groups, the Writing Salon in Toronto, for instance?

Dionne: Not really. At a certain moment in the 1970s, when I came to feminism in a formal way, I met a lot of women writers, including white women writers like Betsy Warland, Gaye Allison, Sarah Sheard, Libby Scheier, and Gwen Hauser.

Pauline: So that writing group constituted a feminist community and not particularly a Black community, although there were Black women in it?

Dionne: Well, the only Black woman in it was Ayanna Black. This was during a time of competing analyses. I didn't feel truly committed to being in a feminist movement that was white. Or that framed itself like that, even though I found these women generous. During my first years in Toronto I had a solid sense of a Black community, in a Black society. It's really weird in the middle of Toronto, but all of my dealings were with Black people, whether it was on campus, in any of my social or political associations, and even economically, because I would find work in the summers with Black organizations and so on. So I was in a completely Black milieu even as we were in a white city. And this moment in the 1970s opened up the possibility of coming to feminism, also coming to that poetry community in Toronto.

Pauline: Makeda (Silvera) wasn't part of the "salon"?

Dionne: No, she wasn't. I think I met Makeda in 1975. She was around earlier but we didn't become friends until about 1975 or so. And then we did various things with other Black writers, like put out pamphlets of poetry.

Pauline: So there were women in the Black community but it just wasn't a "woman-identified" community? Or was it very male?

Dionne: It was very male in its expression, but very female in its practice, as far as who did the work.

Pauline: Typical, eh?

Dionne: Women did everything, like organizing and setting up the meetings. Women made it happen. The men came and gave the speeches. But women handled everything else. There was actually a group called something like "Black Revolutionary Women," a proto-feminist group that Makeda belonged to. I didn't belong to that group. I didn't even know about it until later. Makeda and a few other women had formed it to forward the cause of women within the movement. I was really preoccupied, even obsessed, with writing and writing poetry.

Pauline: What brought you to feminism?

Dionne: I didn't like the position of women in the movement. I was always really wary of it. And just maybe—this is me just thinking about it now—just maybe the fact that I wanted to be a writer and therefore a speaker.

Pauline: Right. You didn't want to be the one just doing the organizing.

Dionne: Well, no. And identifying myself as a writer meant identifying myself as someone who was not going to be sub-jugated, subjected to a certain mode of interaction. I wasn't just going to do the pamphlets. I would do some of that because it was my duty and my obligation and all that. But I think maybe being a writer put me in the position of pulling back a bit and looking at the social organization of the movement. And also I don't think I ever subjected myself to the things that happened to women within those movements, the sexual politics of those movements, like the big shot speaker who has ten women. Male domination scared me. I had a different reaction than a lot of women. I wasn't even out as a lesbian or even knowledgeable of desiring women as a possibility. Male domination just scared me. I wouldn't even have called myself a feminist at that point. Some women are fascinated by male domination, and fascinated by the revolutionary who has all the skills of language in his mouth; the charisma and all the male sexuality that goes along with that. So some women fell into its fascination. But I just got scared.

Pauline: If you had in mind that you wanted to be a writer, then you'd have to find other contexts or communities.

Dionne: Thankfully I knew of women writers who were highly respected, like Nikki Giovanni, Sonia Sanchez, and Gwendolyn Brooks. Those women wrote poetry and were listened to. Albeit some of their poetry was very male-identified, male-affirming poetry for Black men, but there was another quality to it. Nikki Giovanni has a poem about wishing she could write a different kind of poem. She wishes she could write a rhyming poem about trees but realizes that given the reality of her life in the present, more urgent subjects had to be seriously addressed. It was really nice work.

Pauline: How did you come across their work? Through the Black Power movement? Did you hear them read? Did you meet them?

Dionne: No. I heard Nikki Giovanni on a record. And I had heard of Sonia Sanchez. I mean, we were so hungry at seventeen. Here's the Black Power movement and here's rescue. We were so hungry, we just went looking. And people told you to read this book and read that book. There was a real intellectual life, a bookish life. We read Nikki Giovanni as much as we read Franz Fanon's *The Wretched of the Earth*. You had to. This was compulsory reading. As much as *The Communist Manifesto*. These were things you had to read. You read Che [Guevera] you read Fidel [Castro], you read W.E.B. DuBois or Frederick Douglas. This was the re-education of Black human beings. And so of course you did it.

Pauline: That's a fascinating process. At the same time that you're going through university and getting one education, you're also getting another.

Dionne: I know. I never read a Black writer at the University of Toronto. I studied English and Philosophy and I did not read a Black writer unless I suggested it.

Pauline: And then they would be open to it?

Dionne: Yes. I remember having Urjo Kareda in Modern Drama at U of T, and looking at all of this, and saying, yes, Pinter yes, O'Neill yes, all of this. But where the hell is LeRoi Jones [Amira Baraka]? And so I went to him and I said, look, can I do LeRoi Jones for my paper? I'm willing to do all the other reading, but when it comes down to my paper, can I seriously do a Black writer? And he was fine with it. I think he accepted it as long as I didn't say it had to be on the course. And it was not until about 1975 that Fred Case, a Guyanese African in the French Department at U of T, started a course on Black literature. And then of course it's just the one course and it's supposed to cover two continents and an archipelago.

Pauline: Did you take that?

Dionne: Yes. Gobbled it up. Just to be in familiar territory for once.

Pauline: After you graduated from the University of Toronto in the mid-1970s did you go to work?

Dionne: I went to work in a Black organization, the Black Education Project.

Pauline: Does the lesbian community come in then?

Dionne: Oh, much later. I didn't come out until about 1983 or 1984. After Grenada. But feminism began to define the conditions that would make it possible for me to be in the women's movement, that it not only had to satisfy the questions of sex, but it had to deal with questions of race. And if it didn't, I couldn't be a part of it. I continued to work at the magazine, *Spear*, I even edited it. And I continued to write. And so in 1978, I think, my first book came out.

Pauline: Were you at the Women & Words conference in Vancouver in the summer of 1983?

Dionne: Yes, I was. I came back to Canada for three weeks in the summer of 1983 and went to Women & Words.

Pauline: Was that an important event for you?

Dionne: No, not really. I had continued to follow my politics, my left politics to Grenada. I worked in several agencies before that. I worked at the Immigrant Women's Job Placement Centre.

And I was tired from that work, I was really tired. And I wondered, okay, what am I going to do? And then the opportunity came up in Grenada. I didn't yet see writing as my part in the revolution. I still thought other ways of being in a liberation struggle are necessary sometimes. And if you're called, you've got to go. I didn't see writing as a career. I saw its role as making itself available to the liberation. And so I went to Grenada after the revolution in 1979. So while Women & Words was an important moment for feminist writing in Canada, it wasn't the most significant moment for me. I was really still very much involved in doing revolutionary work, and giving myself to it, even as writing had become more and more crucial to me, more and more imperative.

Pauline: And your response to Grenada, interestingly, is *Chronicles of the Hostile Sun*? Your experience in Grenada produced your first major book.

Dionne: Well, actually, I had written the *Winter Epigrams* (1983) and *Primitive Offensive* (1982) just the year before. *Winter Epigrams* I did for myself to see if I could write in the shape of an epigram, which is short and tight and pithy. *Primitive Offensive* was my first attempt at a long piece, the fourth piece in it. So I was starting to figure out how to do this very tight yet fulsome and expressive thing and also this longer thing. But I wanted to figure out how I could do both of them together.

Pauline: Did you feel the longer form allowed more space for the political work that you were involved in? Or was it more a craft issue?

Dionne: I just don't like short poems. I don't think they're sufficient. I mean they can be, when people who can do it well do it well. But I wanted much more speech.

Pauline: The short poem is tied to an aesthetic tradition—as you say in your "Anti-Poetry" poem (*Chronicles* 30–31)—that doesn't allow for very much.

Dionne: Yes. You know, Kamau Braithwaite was at the International Authors' Festival last year and his wife had died and he wrote a long poem, unlike many of his other poems, which are long but spare. And he said he guesses that all of that grief had to fill up and spill out of the page. And that's very close to how I feel about it. What he said just struck me so deeply. That is probably why I like the long poem. There is so much space to fill up and just spill over and over and out and out.

Pauline: And there's so much more than just the individual "I" too, which is what the short poem focuses on.

Dionne: And you can move so much into that poem. When I read Gabriel García Marquez's *One Hundred Years of Solitude* many years ago, it suggested to me just how much could be said. And then I thought of it also in terms of poetry. I saw such possibilities for speech, how you could move in and out of an idea as well as in and out of various voices. I remember reading it and thinking I could write anything.

Pauline: You move in and out of various pronouns, too. Especially in the opening section, "hard against the soul." I presume the "you" is a form of self-address?

Dionne: "this is you girl"?

Pauline: Yes. Is the "you" a form of self-address?

Dionne: Both, maybe.

Pauline: It's very interesting as a writing position, to be addressing "you" instead of speaking as "I," even though the "you" may be the "I." And the "you" can also include someone else.

Dionne: Yes, I'm very wary about using the "you" because it's easy to sound accusatory. And that tone reveals that you're not taking any responsibility in the poem. Somebody else is always doing something. So it's very tricky to use it.

Pauline: Who is the "you" in this line?

Dionne: "this is you girl," that one (*No Language* 6)? I guess that was my first visceral recognition of my sexuality, my lesbian sexuality. I remember driving up this road in the north of Trinidad called Maracas. You go along this almost sheer cliff up to the top of the north coast. You can look down and it just drops. But I suddenly saw the landscape of the place as having to do with my sexuality, that the landscape seemed to me to be female. And even as I say that I know that the land is always feminized.

Pauline: So you were participating in that trope.

Dionne: But I only wanted to record that moment, even as I wanted to reject it. Suddenly it seemed obvious why I had chosen a certain sexuality, why I had chosen what I thought was a certain breadth, to jump out of the confines of things that I had always chafed against so long. This spread, the swell and flow of the land, spoke of possibility. And for a moment I thought, oh, that's why. Because I loved that huge ocean I really wanted to go into the centre of. Loved that rise and fall of everything, and I loved its unity.

Pauline: The sexualized landscape.

Dionne: Yes and no. Because we can't really personify landscape; the land could care less. Yet I was drawn to precisely that—its not belonging to us, its ability to do what we cannot ever expect.

Pauline: So the lesbian community became important after you came back from Grenada?

Dionne: Yes, I talked recently with Margaret Randall about the connection between having gone to Grenada and coming out as a lesbian. I had read the last poem in *Chronicles of the Hostile Sun* at Trinity College in Connecticut. Michelle Cliff had invited me and I didn't realize Margaret was teaching there too. Margaret wrote me a note the night of the reading and slipped it under my door saying she wanted to talk to me about my poem. And we went and talked about it and she said, did I write that poem after Grenada? Because she had come to a lesbian sexuality after Nicaragua. And she said—given where we had situated ourselves, as women needing revolutions, liberation movements—that it blew open for us another thing. And it was very interesting. Because my coming out was after Grenada.

Pauline: You didn't care who you offended?

Dionne: The experience in Grenada had made my perceptions laser sharp. Suddenly it was clear that we had just been playing around with revolution in Toronto, arguing with each other about whether Marx was right. It was just absurd, given the reality in Grenada. I had now seen what could happen, the planes from the skies and the earth just deceiving you and leaving you. Everything you held dear being completely destroyed. We, it seemed to me, had just been joking around, like dilettantes or something. I was doing my M.A. at OISE at the time and I was teaching. I didn't know what to do with myself. I was shell shocked. But I had a course or two to finish, and then the thesis so I sat in on Dorothy Smith's and Dieter Misgeld's course on "The Everyday World as Problematic." But I just couldn't stay. I needed to get up and leave. Not that these people weren't interesting.

Pauline: No, it's the distance between the academy and certain events, isn't it?

Dionne: Yes and I thought to myself, you have nothing to teach me, and you don't know anything. And god knows that wasn't a comment about them, it was the place I was in at that moment.

Pauline: Well, it's a comment about the academy I think, and where it's positioned in relation to other things. What was the subject of your M.A. thesis?

Dionne: Philosophy of Education. My thesis was called "A Conceptual Analysis of how Gender Roles are Racially Constructed." And I just couldn't stand it, I couldn't sit there anymore. I must have needed some explanation of the world after Grenada and that was impossible.

Pauline: What did you do?

Dionne: Well I skipped off for a while and went back to working with women. I went to work at the Immigrant Women's Centre, the health centre, doing abortion counselling and stuff like that. And I co-wrote that book on racism [*Rivers Have Sources, Trees Have Roots*], got into fights with everybody. At that moment I decided I wasn't going to tolerate anything.

———

Pauline: I'd like to return to the question of your relationship to feminism. When you connected to the feminist context in Toronto, what was the springboard for you? Were there particular feminist writers that got you thinking about feminism? I mean as well as your anxiety around male power?

Dionne: Those African American women, actually. Gwendolyn Brooks as well, who was a generation before. She was older than Nikki Giovanni and Sonia Sanchez—but she was available also as a Black writer.

Pauline: Did you read the white feminist theorists like Simone de Beauvoir or Adrienne Rich?

Dionne: Yes, I read Rich's *Of Woman Born*. When did that come out?

Pauline: Mid seventies.

Dionne: I read *Of Woman Born* and I read Shulamith Firestone. Of course as a leftist I read Emma Goldman and people like that. I was always looking for women who could speak. For me, there was always literature and activism. So when I recognized that I would not be able to become a formal speaker in the Black revolutionary movement, I also recognized that I had to do something about it. I just couldn't continue to sit there and do the leaflets. The women writers who were there, or women who wanted to be writers, used to critique and talk about the men in the movement. It wasn't all silence. In fact, there used to be fights too. Not that I was ever part of those fights. But I saw women who were significant figures in the movement, women who could shout the men down, who were very outspoken and loud and would just cuss the men out and tell them about their sexual politics. They would call those men on sexism. But they never did it as a formal part of the movement and they never did it on a public platform. But they had fights, nasty fights, yelling, screaming fights in meetings about how disreputable this man or that man was and what he was doing. Some women were ostracized, expelled from parties. At the same time there was the cultural nationalist movement which said women should walk ten paces behind and all that stuff, and there were women who rejected it. So it wasn't as monolithic as the rally might have looked.

Pauline: I wonder what facilitates that transition from resistance in the back rooms to getting out there and being one of the speakers. That's a big shift isn't it, in terms of social space?

Dionne: At a certain point, some of those women did get to talk. But of course they weren't really listened to. I think the movement did begin to split over things like sexism. Of course, it began to dwindle because of the approach of the state to it, the criminalizing of such activity. But it also began to raise from within questions about sexism. And women withdrew their support and their labour.

Pauline: In your *Kinesis* interview you talk about working coalitionally. You say that the coalitional isn't home. It's a room where you come to negotiate. Would you explain that?

Dionne: I think I was making specific reference to my experience in women's organizations and in the women's movement where I realized that people actually came to these coalitions expecting to be satisfied. But unless we can work through a whole bunch of issues, we're not at a point where we could suggest that it's such a place.

Pauline: Why is this not a "home"? From the way you described your home it was very much like that.

Dionne: I think that after writing *No Language* I realized that home, that whole thing that makes us feel warm and possible or whatever, it's really not something that any of us have experienced. That home is somewhere. If we want we could make it. But it's not something that we've had. And if we think we've had it, that home was probably extremely dysfunctional, because it contained all that was in the world as it is. Those things that we are sometimes struggling against.

Pauline: Right. All the sexism and racism.

Dionne: All the ugly baggage. When we come into a room as feminists we don't always problematize all of those relations.

Pauline: Because we assume we're in a home that's safe?

Dionne: As women, we seem always to want that place, as horrible as it has been for us. I was trying to suggest that we become a little more comfortable with the discomfort of throwing everything up in the air in order to see the possibilities that might become available. I was suggesting that we recognize the ways we can be seduced or tricked into hanging onto old patterns. While recognizing that possibility might also be about loss, I also hoped that in coming together we might be able to construct something else.

Pauline: Yes, I see. Home is not a place of comfort.

Dionne: No, it is a place that needs to be problematized. Home may not be a place where everything's going to be fine. You're not coming into the arms of anything. Maybe then we can figure it out. With this sentimental notion of home in our heads, we expect to come into a room with other feminists and not be upset. That was the situation in Toronto's women's community at that time. I mean, why do you think you can come in here and not be moved, you know? What is it that you are asking us to verify when you ask us not to question you?

Pauline: How do you feel about white women critics writing about your work?

Dionne: I would like more white Canadian critics to read what I read and what people like me read. And to know therefore what we are talking about. What we're bouncing off of, what we're relating to, what we're speaking against and so on. And also to understand that we're not simply speaking against some thing, some concept called racism. We're also not speaking about some concept called the Black experience. No one writer writes about the "white" experience and nobody titles it that way. So I would like them to read Taban Lo Liyong and I'd like them to read Sonia Sanchez and I'd like them to read Ayi Kwei Armah and I'd like them to read…

Pauline: Who's that last one?

Dionne: The Ghanian writer, he's a novelist (*The Beautyful [sic] Ones Are Not Yet Born*). I'd like them to read a whole variety of literature that I have read, like Aimé Césaire. I'd like them to read Kamau Braithwaite, I'd like them to read Derek Walcott, I'd like them to read Martin Carter, I'd like them to read George Lamming, I'd like them to read Edgar Mitzleholtzu, Jacques Romain. I could name each continent. You know, Toni Cade Bambara, Gayle Jones, Charles Johnson. I'd like them to read all of these writers. I'd like them to read nineteenth-century African American women writers. Because I read and respond to all of these writers. It's the world I'm living in. And I'd also like them to read themselves. That is, I'd like them to read what's missing when they write. And what's missing when they write about white writers who live in the same place as I do. I want them to write me into it. How does it work? How is it possible for a white writer in downtown Toronto to write what he or she writes?

Pauline: Especially if it's totally excluding…

Dionne: And when it does include, how does it include. Does it do it well? Does it do it badly? I'd like them to engage white Canadian writers in the business of how to live where we are living, as much as they engage me about how I'm living where I'm living.

———

Pauline: Your work takes many forms—poetry, fiction, essays, film, oral histories. What got you interested in doing oral history?

Dionne: I wanted to write a book in the voices of those people who could tell about racism in Canada, so that they would not be disputed in some way. It wouldn't simply be my opinion. It was actually people talking about what happened to them today and

yesterday and the day before and the year before last and twenty
years ago, and how it had constructed their lives and so on. And
I wanted that to be plain. Also at that time racism wasn't clearly
acknowledged. You felt like it sort of happened but it didn't
really happen and you're told in the public discourse you're
misinterpreting what's happening. So I wanted a hundred voices,
two hundred voices saying these things.

Pauline: You wanted documents.

Dionne: Yes. I thought that if I could facilitate that documentation
then that's fine too. That's also my job. But again, it's also this
business of activism and writing that constructs the form in a
way. I don't know how I decide these things, I really don't.

Pauline: Well, that makes sense when you say it's the relationship
between activism and writing that produces the form. If it's these
particular voices that you want to be heard then it takes the form
of documentary. If it's some kind of visual representation, it
draws you into film, and so on.

Dionne: It's also a kind of interaction with the cultural life or
the social milieu. At the point of film, I wasn't even going to
be directing films or anything like that. I just wanted to see
something of the book represented. I had met these women and
some of them were so wonderful. And then an opportunity came
along at Studio D, where I was asked to collaborate on another
film with a white woman about racism. And after sitting with
her for several days and talking with her about what she wanted
to do—she was the filmmaker and I was consulting—I realized
I didn't want to work on that at all. That it was a whole other
agenda that I really didn't want to work on. And I told the studio,
look, if you ever want to do something about Black women from
their point of view, about their life, about their history, there's
lots to do, if you want that then call me. The film *Long time
comin'* was the result.

Pauline: Do you have a sense of different audiences for those
different pieces? Is that partially why you use different forms?

Dionne: The oral histories I've done came about because there
weren't many history books on working-class women from
the 1920s to the 1940s. Winks' *The Blacks in Canada*, written
in the 1960s and published in 1971, was the central, defining
tome. And ever since then, no reputable press has done any kind

of comprehensive work.* So I thought, this is important, and I don't really care if an academic press does it. It needs to be done and I'll do it, I'll get a project together somehow and get these interviews done and so on. I should mention another book that I've co-authored: *We're Rooted Here and They Can't Pull Us Up: essays in African Canadian Women's History* (1994). Peggy Bristow was the co-ordinator and the co-authors were Adrienne Shadd, Afua Cooper, Linda Carty, Sylvia Hamilton and myself. We didn't see this as the definitive work. We took Black women's history and did five essays on particular periods.

Pauline: You said last night that you were so relieved that you were writing poetry again.

Dionne: Some writing is a duty, some a pleasure.

Pauline: Writing poetry is a pleasure?

Dionne: Oh yes. I'm extremely unhappy if I don't write poetry. If I wanted my life represented, and if I could choose a shape for its representation, I would choose poetry. It's not that other shapes wouldn't be interesting and important, because we live in a society where things take many shapes. I feel I have to address all those shapes too. A lot of young Black women have seen the film I've worked on and they say to me, oh, I really loved that. I sense their relief and thankfulness at being able to watch themselves or people like themselves in a film. And I recognize film as a modern medium. A lot more young people go to films than read. But if I want my life represented in its fullness and its beauty then it takes the shape of poetry.

---

* A second edition of *The Blacks in Canada* was printed in 1997, after this interview was completed.

five "I make sense of my world through writing"

AN INTERVIEW WITH MARIE ANNHARTE BAKER

Interviewed by Pauline Butling

MARIE ANNHARTE BAKER, FIRST NATIONS POET, ESSAYIST, ACTIVIST, performer, dramatist, and mixed media artist was born in Winnipeg in 1942 to an Irish father and Anishinabe mother. She uses her middle name, Annharte (a Welsh name from a character in the movie *How Green Is My Valley*), as her author name because the character in the movie offers hope for poor people. She started writing out of a "quiet imperative" to speak out for herself and other marginalized subjects ("Marie Annharte Baker" 63). She "make[s] sense of [her] world through writing" because she finds the "enemy" is "within one's own language use and how one is programmed to look at things" ("Borrowing" 59) and further that "writing is a way...to be sane in this society" ("Borrowing" 61).

Annharte grew up in Winnipeg but often spent summer holidays with her Anishinabe grandparents on the reserve in the Interlake Region of Manitoba. In the 1960s, she attended Brandon College (1963–65), the University of British Columbia, and Simon Fraser University. But she describes these years as "failures" in the sense that educational institutions did not provide her with relevant or useful knowledge. She educated herself by extensive reading and talking with people, a process that began in high school out of boredom and continued in her adult life out of necessity. More useful in terms of formal education were her classes at the University of Minnesota in the 1970s, the Red Deer College Summer School of Writing in 1988 (where she worked with bpNichol), her studies at the University of Winnipeg in the early 1990s, and her summer at the Naropa Summer Institute on Pan American and Eco-Poetics in 1992. In 1995 she received a B.A. in English from the University of Winnipeg.

Her community activist work began in the 1960s, starting with a summer job at the Native Friendship Centre in Winnipeg in 1963. She started going to the National Indian Youth Council gatherings in the U.S. and became a founding member of the Canadian Indian Youth Council. In Vancouver in the 1960s she joined the Native Alliance for Red Power. She has also worked on various projects designed to improve the life of urban Indians and has been active in several writing groups, including the Aboriginal Writers' Group in Regina in the 1980s and the Carnegie Centre Writing Group in Vancouver in the 1990s. Her studies and work have taken her to numerous places in Canada and the United States, including Ottawa, Vancouver, Minneapolis-St. Paul, Milwaukee, Regina, and Vancouver. She has a son, Forrest Funmaker, and three grandchildren.

Annharte began writing in high school but did not publish until the 1980s. With the publication of her first book, *Being on the Moon* (1990), she emerged as a major figure in the articulation of race and gender issues and in the development of an innovative race poetics. In *Being on the Moon*, the lyric line—along with reductive race and gender constructs—is unhinged by witty word play: "I often race to write   I write about race   why do I write / about race   I must erase all trace of my race   I am an / eraser abrasive bracing myself embracing" ("Raced Out to Write this Up" *Being* 60). Based on thirteen moons that reflect women's menstrual cycles, each of the thirteen sections consists of five poems that are loosely connected to a common theme, indicated in the first poem of each section. "Scribble Moon," is the first in a series of five poems that have to do with writing. "Hooker Moon" begins a cluster on women's sexuality. The "Cheeky Moon" section focuses on stories of survival and resistance. Peter Dickinson credits Baker with an innovative adaptation of the Indigenous tradition of "'storytelling cycles'" into written form (Dickinson 335). Baker likewise emphasizes the link to oral storytelling traditions, describing the poems as stories about ordinary people and situations, stories that have been lost because of the erasure and/or silencing of Native people ("Author's Note" 368). While anger fuels many of the poems, wit and humour ruffle their surfaces, at once lightening and intensifying their political bite.

Annharte's work throughout the 1990s continues to combine wit, humour, satire, and storytelling in an ongoing critique of the effects of colonization. In "Albeit Original," a play performed at the Edmonton Popular Theatre Festival and Toronto's Nightwood Theatre's Groundswell Festival in 1994, she creates grandmother stories for the two main characters (Coyote Girl and Rat Lady). The stories help them combat the effects of cultural appropriation because they provide "'medicine lines' that connect us" ("Medicine Lines: The Doctoring of Story and Self" 117). In *Coyote Columbus Cafe* (1994), she focuses as much on taking apart the "discovery" narratives as on recovering First Nations stories. The title poem sets the comic/satiric tone of the book as she mocks both the colonizers—"Columbus did lack / cultural awareness" (14)—and the colonized: "discover an authentic Indian colonizer / slaver inside you" (16). The titles of other poems in the collection show Annharte's continuing witty critique: "Tongue in Cheek, if not Tongue in Check," "Columbus Circumscribed," and "Discovery Two." Annharte notes in an essay on "Borrowing Enemy Language," that "wit" is often her main tool in her "arsenal of word weapons" (61). "Coyote Columbus Cafe" ends on an up-beat note, with the poet claiming a place "on the totem pole": "if I am to be tokenized / or totemized / I'd rather become / more a totem than token / I end up doing the work / don't get a free ride / I deserve my place / on the totem pole" ("The Poet Wishes to be Totem" 48).

A third poetry collection, *Blueberry Canoe*, was announced in 2001 but did not appear. Annharte withdrew the manuscript in order to revise it. It became *Exercises in Lip Pointing* (2003), a collection of hard-hitting, mostly narrative poems that often speak the unspeakable in terms of violence, injustices, and abuses of power against First Nations people, especially in the middle section, titled "Red Noise." The first section, "Memory Fishes," starts off with a happy memory, "a rainbow arcs over busy aunties"

("Auntie I Dream" 4) but gradually moves into darker tones as the poet recalls "the hole in her memory when her mother left" ("Blueberry Canoe" 7), or when she "tallied up total of all conquests except the total of me equals none" ("Cherries Could Be a Girl's Best" 9). The last section, titled "Coyotrix Recollects," extends the theme of remembering with poems that intermingle contemporary and historical situations. In "Squaw Pussy" she counters the "Hollywood Indian princesses / with braids & dowdy looks" (22) with a stylish, contemporary First Nations woman driving a Jaguar. In the final poem, "Red Stone Lake," she reiterates the restorative role of storytelling in likening the story to a stone: "stones incubate promise / sanctuary / stay for / coming home ceremony" (86).

Annharte has published two essays: "Medicine Lines" and "I Make Sense of My World Through Writing." Her poetry has been anthologized in *Visit Tepee Town: Native Writings After the Detours* (Glancy and Nowak 1999), *An Anthology of Native Canadian Literature in English* (Moses and Goldie 1992), *Miscegenation Blues: Voices of Mixed Race Women* (Camper 1994), *Uncommon Wealth: An Anthology of Poetry in English* (Besner et al. 1997), and *Native Poetry in Canada: A Contemporary Anthology* (Armstrong and Grauer 2001). For critical discussions of her work see Peter Dickinson, "Orality in Literacy: Listening to Indigenous Writing"; Lally Grauer, "'The weasel pops in and out of old tunes': Marie Annharte Baker as a Scavenger Poet"; and Reg Johanson's review of *Exercises in Lip Pointing*.

five

Pauline Butling: I'd like to begin with a very basic question: why did you start writing?

Annharte: Well, there were lots of reasons, but one was that I wanted to live as a writer. I wanted to have an interesting life. When I was in High School, I began reading about writers who had interesting lives, like the women in Paris—Colette for instance. I wanted to be adventurous and they seemed to model a kind of freedom, they could be intellectual but they could also be sensual. They could also have a life of their own—they didn't have to be married. That's what I wanted. I also read about Greenwich Village in New York City, that's where I wanted to be. I wanted to be like the American women that were living and writing in this kind of bohemian situation. I did NOT want to be in Winnipeg. I wanted to be in a place where women were celebrated for their minds.

Pauline: When did you actually start writing?

Annharte: My first conscious attempt to write was in the 1960s when I was going to Simon Fraser University. I was taking a class that had *The Communist Manifesto* as a text, so I wrote a "Manifesto for First People." If only I had a copy of that now, I would love to be able to compare what I thought then to what I think now. I'd also been writing some poetry then. I had attempted to keep a diary as a teenager, but because one particular thing happened—I experienced a date rape—I ended up burning them all. That was in the fifties, in high school. I wrote a poem a little while ago about how that event silenced my wanting to write about myself. I felt I had betrayed myself. I took a lot of responsibility for being in a situation that made me vulnerable. When I look back I think it was because I was with another Native woman. I had some privilege in dating because I had fair skin so I would not be taken for a Native woman just by sight. But in this case, because I was with her, we were both mistreated. I felt I should have been smarter, I should have known this could happen to me. There was no way to report this to the police, it was really difficult. As a result I hurt myself more. I felt the wound wasn't even the rape; it was when I burnt the diaries. In a recent poem I tried to take the images that I had in the diary. I did other retrieval poems too, I did one that was modeled on a cockroach. I was thinking okay, I can make it around society because I'm light-skinned, but once you say you're First Nations you're an outcast, or low caste, underclass. You have the whole stigma and shame that has been put on Native people. I became quite aware of that, so I wrote about how durable the cockroach was. I was placing my faith in the idea that no matter how low you would go, there was something resilient to draw on. I wish I could find that poem now.

Pauline: Were you influenced or inspired by any particular writers?

Annharte: Well if I told you which writers interested me you'd think it was strange. I think of it as funny now. I liked anything to do with humour, so one Canadian writer I liked was Stephen Leacock. But then I switched straight away to Richard Armour. He wrote short, funny poems that I liked. Somehow I found his poetry in the library. Nobody had ever told me about him. And then I found another humorist—I don't remember his name—but he wrote about a cockroach called Archie and a cat called Mehitabel that had taken over a newspaper office at night. And the cockroach would write about the cat. The cat was a role model that I liked. She was a free thinker, and she had her bad love affairs, meeting all sorts of tomcats and that kind of thing. I was also reading some earlier French writers, like de Maupassant and Émile Zola. And I remember reading something by Eudora Welty that I really liked, about a Mexican woman who gave her all. She ended up killing her boyfriend's girlfriend or something like that. I thought that was really hot stuff because you never saw that. We weren't finding images of ourselves. This was about a Mexican woman and it had a lot of passion in it.

Pauline: You lived in Vancouver for several years in the 1960s. What drew you to Vancouver?

Annharte: When I dropped out of Brandon College, I went to Ottawa to work as a student organizer. I met some students there from The University of British Columbia that I really liked because I liked their politics. So many people wanted to "save" us. But the UBC students weren't just feeling sorry for the "poor Indian." I was also pregnant and decided to have my baby in Vancouver since it was closer to my ex-husband, father of my child. He lived in California.

Pauline: What did you study at UBC?

Annharte: I went there to study Anthropology and I took a course with Wilson Duff, but I hated it. He used the traditional, British approach to Anthropology, which was to put everything into categories, rather than the American approach, which was more interactive. The way Duff talked about the Indian was very demeaning. You got the impression that Indians were an inferior class. I was always challenging him, questioning him, like the character Marie in Sherman Alexie's novel *Indian Killer*.

Pauline: When did you get involved with the Red Power movement? Was that when you were in Vancouver?

Annharte: It was earlier than that, when I got involved with the Canadian Indian Youth Council. I got a summer job with the CIYC in 1963, when I was still in Winnipeg. We started going to meetings of the National Indian Youth Council in the States. That's kind of why I eventually dropped out of Brandon College. College became quite irrelevant once I began educating myself about the world. Before that I had thought I could get an education from books. Then I started educating myself by meeting people. Later on, in Vancouver, I got involved with the Native Alliance for Red Power. But it was led by a white Trotskyite and I didn't like the idea of white guys running things, nor the idea that women would just do the drudge work. I wanted to be a speaker not a secretary. I remember a poem that I wrote then that I'd love to have now—I called it "Mr. Indian." I was becoming aware of how First Nations people were putting on a show for white people. That's what "Mr. Indian" in my poem was doing. He'd put on his bolo tie and talk to the Canadian press about Indian people. And as soon as the mike was taken away from him he reverted to something else. He was no longer "Mr. Indian."

Pauline: In the title poem in *Coyote Columbus Cafe* there's a comic/satiric voice that jokes about "The Indian Act" as a performance, that Indians have to act the part, as well as be ruled by the legal Act. Is this related to your idea of performing the role of the Indian?

Annharte: Oh definitely. In fact I was just looking at that poem this morning because I thought I might read it at the reading today. I don't know if people get this kind of humour. Even if you haven't read any Indian history, you can kind of figure it out:

> *lo, the po' Indian*
>
> *Indian Act*
> *Tell Old Indian joke*
> *like Indian Affairs*
>
> *Act Indian*
> *had an Indian affair lately?*
> ("Coyote" 15, rpt. in Armstrong and Grauer 75)

There's a compressed humour that has evolved over thirty or forty years about the name of the government agency, Indian Affairs, and about the Indian Act. A woman came up to me once when I was doing a performance and asked me when I got interested in theatre and the first thing that popped into my mind was well, there's the Indian "Act." We were all forced to be actors in some strange way. The joke about Indian Affairs became a huge laugh for Indian people.

Pauline: I really enjoy the humour in your work.

Annharte: Well good, because I feel a lot of people don't understand my jokes. When I'm reading to a room of people, every once in a while I see someone whose eyes light up, their expression is aglow and they seem to be affected bodily by my reading. But I don't hear the ruckus I'd like to hear.

Pauline: What is the appeal of humour for you?

Annharte: Well, anger is a tag that's always put on First Nations' writing. I feel it's often a way to dismiss it because it just means that the person is hearing with the ears of a white person. If you listen from the perspective of a First Nations person, you may hear anger but you definitely go for the humour. It's not because the anger is so uncomfortable, it's just that it seems to be part of the whole "Indian Act."

—

Pauline: I'd like to talk about *Being on the Moon* now. When were these poems written?

Annharte: I would say I started writing them twelve years before I published the book. A lot of it was written when I was in Ontario. I had a job as a social worker to save Native children from the grasp of social service agencies. I worked in Dryden and Sioux Lookout. So I spent a lot of time by myself driving, and this was where some of the poems came from. I wrote poems to keep myself company.

Pauline: The poems were written over a period of several years then?

Annharte: Yes, if you're talking about process as opposed to actually writing things down. At one point I sent some out to magazines. I had found some poems in the bottom of a closet that were written when I had just lost a job. I typed them up and thought, I've got nothing to lose, so I sent them out. One of them went to *Contemporary Verse 2* in Winnipeg. And lucky for me, Kristjana Gunnars was one of the editors at that time. She liked my "Moon Bear" poem and she wrote to me saying, "Do you have any more like this?" And I sent her others but I don't think she liked any of those so I believe that was the only one that was published there (*Being on the Moon* 19). Later on I did get some others published in *Prairie Fire*. But before then, maybe six months before, my first publication of a poem was in New

York. I always think that was kind of nice. The magazine was called *Conditions, Conditions* 13. I think. They published the one about my experience as a shoplifter ("Hudson's Bay Bill" *Being on the Moon* 33). That was based on my losing my credit card at the Hudson's Bay store. I wrote the poem about what they owed me. That was fun, I was learning then to deal with some of the injustices in written form.

Pauline: You have said that *Being on the Moon* was based on thirteen moons, that you were trying to establish your own calendar.

Annharte: Yes, right. But at first I had only written the "Moon Bear" poem and it was quite a painful experience to write that. When I sent the poem to my woman friend in the States she said why don't you write twelve more? Me, write twelve more moon poems! But then I went to the Red Deer writing school [Red Deer College Summer Writing Workshop, 1988]. That's when I wrote more of them. I met bpNichol there. The first thing he put in my mind was that I could have a book. I thought okay, maybe. I remember I had called one of my sections "Being on the Moon." The idea of a book struck me as an interesting challenge and so I decided to try to make a calendar, which represented something of myself, but also related to other Native people's calendars. I looked at several: Haida, Cree, Ojibway. I looked at these calendars and thought, okay this fits here, and that's how I came up with my arrangement.

Pauline: Do the poems record different times of the year, or different kinds of experiences?

Annharte: I was very conscious of my period at the time—when I think back I was probably entering menopause and didn't know it—I was having severe PMS attacks. When I had my period it was like being taken out for a good week of the month. So the calendar became very important as a symbol of my own body and also as a reaching out to other women. One of the poems was written in a hospital waiting room when I was undergoing a heavy PMS attack. I could barely sit still. I wanted to be in about ten places at once, I was spinning. So that particular poem catches that feeling of pressure and that there is nothing in the world that will alleviate it. I turned to the idea of a grand-mother moon who, for some reason, has arranged for us to be fertile, even when we don't want to be. Writing that poem was like making my own medicine. I was curing myself because the poem remained with me. Whenever I would get like that I could say, "Oh yeah, I remember." The poem became a personal friend/advisor.

Pauline: The poems explore some experiences that must have been hard to write about?

Annharte: Once I started getting into the stuff I really liked it. I started getting off on it because I felt more connected to writing. I remember reading poetry when I was in one of my phases of being a battered woman, this was when I was married. I used to go to the university library and read and read. This was one of my only solaces, being in a world where words counted and they were beautiful. They weren't lies, which was what I was experiencing in my relationship. I learned to associate poetry with this place of protection, a place of safety.

Pauline: Is that why you can bring difficult content into it?

Annharte: Yes, because I'm in my safe place. I figured if you go to the moon and you look down, you're a very powerful person because you've already got up there.

Pauline: Let's talk about form for a moment: Many of the poems in *Being on the Moon* take off in several directions and don't always make connections.

Annharte: Oh, I love that!

Pauline: So do I. Would you talk about how this disjunctive process works for you.

Annharte: It's like my mind is a racing car, things just flood over me. I'm quite overwhelmed. Like this one ("Granny Going" *Being on the Moon* 15)—it's based on a real experience of helping someone who was hitchhiking, giving her a ride. She was trying to get her back to her family. I picked the details that I liked, like the fact that she had a plastic garbage bag that she had made to look like a backpack. I thought that was wonderful. I also liked the idea that she was going off to take a sixty-mile walk in the bush. I thought wow, that's awesome. I felt even a bit overwhelmed by her. So I think there's a bit of that feeling of being overwhelmed in the poem. But there's also a process of sketching. That's what I see now. I was sketching. I didn't need to fill in a lot of details. I also like to push things to the end of the line. I see it as a kind of cliff, with everything pushed over, falling over into the next line, and again and again. "Raced Out to Write this Up" (*Being on the Moon* 60) is a poem where it's very hard to breathe. In fact I always go panting away in it.

Pauline: Yes, it's one long riff, as they say in jazz.

Annharte: What about this one? That's when I really tried the sketching thing:

> at night… you get dark feelings… for a dark lover… at day-time it goes… darkloving… gives anyone… a cherry… abc teachers… do it at my office… do it in school… streets are free… boozecans charge so much… crazy talk seductions… need figuring out… eyes wink wild… them bellies lean on me… tonight will come so slow… save it my love… stretch my reach… chalk up this… charming my words… no fumbles at sex… boarding school boyfriend look alike… same jokes crack… look down on me…white lying… so I'm chiefless… remind me
>
> ("Dark Love" *Being on the Moon* 35)

Pauline: In "Borrowing Enemy Language," the paper you gave at the Inglish Writing with an Accent conference, you talked about how language itself is an instrument of colonization. Here's the section I'm thinking of:

> When I speak of English as the enemy's language, I see the enemy as being *within* the individual person—within one's own language use and how one is programmed to look at things. Those who see only the enemy outside are, fortunately foolish, because it's more difficult to detect the enemy within. A second language, or even one's first or mother tongue, might be the hiding place for a racist ideology. I do think of myself as a "word warrior" because I have to fight with words that demean my experience as an indigenous person…. I make sense of my world through writing. If a writer does not question imposed language, then, to me, this writer is only passing on oppression to the reader or listener—we are hearing the "colonized Native" voice. (61 Annharte's emphasis)

Pauline: Would you say more about how you "make sense of your world through writing."

Annharte: I do it by naming things and by using the vernacular, which has an immediacy. Street language is not language that's usually written down, but that's the language you have to use to survive. I also do it by taking on the language that makes you feel lesser than what you are, like a native person has an English voice living in them. You have to take on that language. I do it by joking, by taking on bureaucratic words. It's an Indian conversational device. To joke about words is a way to deprogram ourselves.

Pauline: Let's look at how this works in "Coyote Columbus Cafe." How do humour and wordplay help to deprogram the colonized Indian in that poem?

Annharte: Well, we have to go with what we're exposed to and I was exposed to a lot of street language so I sometimes use crude or rude words. Most of the words I use are like colours on an artist's palette. Some words suggest darker meanings, or might be considered gross or impolite. To me, that's perfect for poetry.

Pauline: In this book you play around with words a lot, often taking a familiar phrase or story and changing it a bit to show aspects of colonialism. Here's an example: in the very first stanza you take words from a well-known English children's song, "Pop goes the weasel" and rearrange them:

1. **once more it's Indian time**

   always good to be
   born the midnight star
   500 night years ago
   quincentennial dawn
   time worth waiting for
   never a dull moment
   time circles
   how a weasel pops
   in & out of old tunes
   ("Coyote," rpt. in Armstrong and Grauer 71)

Pauline: In the context of the Columbus quincentennial, the image of the weasel popping "in & out of old tunes" suggests to me the deception and trickery in colonial discourses. Is that what you were thinking of?

Annharte: To me the weasel popping gives the idea of surprise. Nothing is predictable as it is in an old tune or nursery rhyme. I was also thinking that colonial time is always linear. I'm suggesting that time is circular, which is a Native concept. Time occurs in cycles and patterns. I'm also questioning the supposed onset of a new era. Now everything is supposed to be different for native peoples. Many Native people think that we're already decolonized.

Pauline: But you're still governed by the Indian Act!

Annharte: Yes, but many people don't see that.

Pauline: In the next section, you start playing with the meaning of "bar" and "grill" in the phrase "my favourite bar and grill" turning the nouns into verbs —"I bar none / grill some." Is that another example of deprogramming?

Annharte: Perhaps. I've always been aware that when speaking English to a Native audience, most speakers will salt and pepper their talk with wordplay. It's a storytelling method. It's a kind of pause, to give people time to catch up. I also enjoy working with the sounds of words. But I was also thinking of what goes on between people, when you're trying to talk to someone or flirting or whatever, you're still trying to get past the obvious rejection of you as a native person. So there's this sense of "grilling" someone in the sense of what are their attitudes towards native people.

Pauline: How does the wordplay help to resist oppression?

Annharte: It's like with the storyteller's pause, which says "Are you all with me now?" Or when you're in a room talking and you pause for a moment and look at people to see if they're connecting to you. Are they accepting what you're saying? Are they going to let you say a bit more? The wordplay eases the blow.

Pauline: What meanings are you playing with in: "Boozho dude. Hey, I'm talking/ to you. Bozo Dude. My name is / Conquista. Come on adore me" (Armstrong and Grauer 71).

Annharte: I'm joking with the word "bojous." That's an Ojibway expression for something like, "How are you?" Some people think there's a link to the French "bonjour." Others say there's

a link to the trickster Nanabozo. When people started going to
cultural awareness sessions, some native terms became popular
and some native people would begin by saying "boozo" to the
audience. The joke, by turning it into bozo, is just to play with
the word: maybe the person you're going to speak to isn't that
sensitive to what you're going to talk about.

Pauline: "Bozo" is almost an insult?

Annharte: Yes, or a teasing remark. Again, it's customary for Native
people to play around with words. It's a kind of minimizing of the
speaker, a kind of leveling in terms of who you're speaking to.

Pauline: Doesn't it also empower the speaker?

Annharte: Right, because you're turning it around. But with Native
people when you're joking with them or teasing them, this is a
way to start a dialogue, as opposed to putting on a pompous air.
Humour introduces an informality.

Pauline: Let's look at the second section:

2. what does a poor coyote girl do?

I act choosy about what abuse
my clientele gets
I am the first one got Coyotisma
(dey all say dey ever met one)
if they don't like dis talk
I do tease 'em up to the climax
of my act but I am too damn direct
for the colonized coyote
poor oppressed critter

> *hey, you on the Columbus trip*

even when I yell at them
I get the usual ho hum complaint
as Coyotrix I lie and trick
what does a poor coyote girl do?

sure I pose baffling questions
administer random coyote IQ tests

> *what is paler than stranger?*

(Armstrong and Grauer 72)

Pauline: You say that "as Coyotrix, I lie and trick"—is trickery one of your strategies for turning things around? Is Coyotrix the poet?

Annharte: Yes, Coyotrix is my term. I wanted to make up my own supreme authority, and one of them I called Creatrix. I have it in another poem where she works in a lab, etc. In fact I even made a lab coat and wore it to several readings. But when I looked at the other aspects, I chose Coyotrix—I guess it represents all the trickster tendencies. This particular claim—"what does a poor coyote girl do?"—is usually what people say when they see something that they can't really change. The trickster part of it is to create baffling questions. I think what I'm joking about is that method, that everything is baffling. My work has some strange ideas in it, which cause puzzlement. I guess that's the value in it, not to take everything so literally. I try to get away from the authoritarian aspect of being the author.

Pauline: I like your humorous treatment of the question of political correctness, as in the lines: "Columbus did lack / cultural awareness / equity / affirmative action / political correctness" (73). Again, you take standard phrases and play with them and in this case laugh at them.

Annharte: Well yeah, and particularly with the onset of the quincentennial. As far as I was concerned no one was really getting at some of these issues of who made history, or even who made science for that matter—all these questions of knowledge—because they were just glossing over everything and again re-affirming the idea that okay, Natives are here now in North America and South America and so what. There wasn't much questioning of the responsibility to know one's history.

Pauline: You use a two-column form throughout this poem, and in some cases two distinct voices as well? One voice seems friendly and colloquial; the next one seems quite different. Here's an example:

3. Discovery is a hard act to follow

Colon would get comforted
by a kindly Native who'd say

> *Don't feel bad bro.*
> *You're lost like the rest of us.*

if Columbus was looking for turkey
he came to the right place

he'd get the deserved treatment
join our healing process

> *Do you feel like a wounded
> buffalo raging within?*

mine's ready & raring to stampede
right over a cliff
(73)

Pauline: Why do you use two voices?

Annharte: I anticipate some denial of my questioning of the Columbus story. I figure I will have already ticked people off. They didn't expect all these quotes of genocide, how many people were killed. And then there's this ironic fact that there would probably be a Native person—even though this horrendous history has happened—who would comfort a mass murderer like Columbus and say *"[d]on't feel bad bro. / You're lost like the rest of us."* That's one of the amazing contradictions, especially within our own communities, that there's sometimes an incredible forgiveness for oppressors, but less tolerance or patience for victims. I guess I'm re-instating the idea that we are sometimes so colonized in our thinking we're not even aware that this happened to us and that this guy's name "Colon" is part of that actual word colonized.

Pauline: So the double columns emphasize different meanings or different positions?

Annharte: Oh definitely. I thought of them showing a speaker who's in this setting and who would shift between comforting the colonizer and then switching to *"Do you feel like a wounded / buffalo raging within?"*—that's the language of a healing circle. I guess I'd say I'm tightening the screw a little bit more, suggesting that a person like Columbus could even be invited to a healing circle, that somebody would say, "Oh yeah, he could get help there." It's so easy now for people to go to healing circles. Even policemen go. There's this almost magical belief that some transformation will happen. I guess I have a juxtaposition there when the speaker says "*Do you feel like a wounded / buffalo raging within?*" then shifts right away to "mine's ready & raring to stampede / right over a cliff" (73). I get at the rage—that's how Native people ended up hunting the buffalo, by stampeding them over cliffs—and at the contradiction of the buffalo being killed and killing itself. I was trying to introduce the idea that underneath it all is this incredible rage that we all feel. But doing it in a bit of a poking way to the reader. Not doing the build-up. Trying to get a bit of empathy but still not allowing the overwhelming sadness, the false pity.

Pauline: Further on, the double columns sound like sober and drunk talk, for example in the lines "I said sweat lodge / makes body clean inside" on one side and on the other, "*I shed shwatch ludge / meks buddy kleen insaid*" (Armstrong and Grauer 74).

Annharte: That part is not so much drunk talk, it's more an imitation (like Kinsella's) of the way the "uneducated" Indian talks. Some of it is close to actual speech, but I push it a little more. It amused me. Like with the word "Zjoonias," which means money, I exaggerate the pronunciation ("Sch-oo-nash") to emphasize the sort of conspiratorial talk where an elder is saying, "hey we could make money off this":

Zjoonias, my boy. Think of it.	*Sch-oo-nash, my bah. Tinkobit.*
Swiss bank account, hey boy!	*Swish bank a cunt, heh bah!*
(75)	

Pauline: You push it even further with "Swish bank a cunt." The exaggeration achieves the same turn-around that you've created throughout the poem; you expose the exploitation. That kind of wordplay works really well for me.

Annharte: Again, this is a narrative device of a storyteller. They would exaggerate how a person talks to get a laugh. This actually comes from a talk in my creative writing class. We had a policeman in the class who told us he was going to a sweat lodge. I was horrified. He didn't understand that just putting a big toe into Indian culture was really going to take him over the falls so to speak.

Pauline: Is that what you mean by "culture vulture voyeur trips" (75)?

Annharte: I was trying to get at how was a policeman going to a sweat lodge going to bring about social change. How do you deal with the oppressiveness that some learn when they get to be authority figures—like policemen, social workers, nurses, etc. They've been given these ideas about society and how they're supposed to enforce the rules. Then someone says we're going to a sweat lodge, and I thought, no, you don't get deprogrammed that easily.

Pauline: In storytelling, reversals and exaggerations are used mainly for humour. But in your poems, they also seem to be part of a strong social critique.

Annharte: Yes, and self-critique too. In this case, I visioned a kind of twilight zone—one of those odd places where people meet—where all of a sudden a person would be made aware of the history, of what's happening now, what's possible in the future, what kind of time whirl we're in. Obviously people do get an opportunity to talk and become aware of racism. I was also thinking about how circular this whole process can be, this adventure of "discovering" things. With the wannabees, sometimes you have to say, "Oops you've overdone it, too much discovery!" You'd assume that as with friends you'd be discovering things together. But with the wannabe person, you get the impression that they're going to roll you under with this steamroller of new knowledge that they have.

Pauline: In the last line of this section—"how does a coyote girl get / a tale outta her mouth?" (76)—I presume you're referring to Native stories being stifled by the colonizers or by the wannabees. Is this a sexual reference too?

Annharte: I guess so, but I was thinking of the coyote chasing its tale. Also, I made this particular speaker a bit of a slut because I wanted that voice to come out more. Native women seem shy and quiet until they get drunk and then that voice would come out and all the forbidden things were spoken.

———

Pauline: Can we talk a little bit about *Exercises in Lip Pointing*, which seems to me to be very different from your other books. Each of them has a distinct compositional method. *Being on the Moon* seems fast-paced, lyrical, with a lot of language-play. In

Coyote Columbus Cafe there's even more wordplay, but it's also more narrative, or maybe I should say anti-narrative because you take apart the "discovery" narratives. In *Exercises*, I see more narrative and more direct anger. Why do you use more narrative in this book?

Annharte: It was probably because I was doing more work in drama and storytelling. *Being on the Moon* had more of what I would call sketches. In *Coyote Columbus Cafe*, I was exploring things more, allowing myself to circle back in the poem, kind of traversing the area a few times. With *Exercises in Lip Pointing*, when I first read through the published book, I was surprised at the depth of despair in it and also the struggle to come back up. To actually experience some of those painful feelings, you have to face them, or just feel the pain for a while. In parts of the book I'm taking an audience through that process. I was also surprised at the shock value of some of the poems, how hard-hitting they were.

Pauline: Does that go back to your earlier statement about using the vernacular as a way of deprogramming?

Annharte: To some extent yes, but in other ways, it's to just make people more aware of things. For instance, "JJ Bang Bang" (44–50) goes back to the personal despair I felt about that particular tragedy, but I'm also hyping it a bit because I felt it was odd that hardly anyone had written a poem about J.J. Harper and what happened.* So I definitely added some volume and impact there to make it more hard-hitting. I'm creating the police person to be like a monster, like a Nazi, to convey what it's like to feel powerless on the street when there's this particular person who has all the power.

Pauline: And that kind of oppression is enacted on the body. It's a physical experience, hence the crude language?

* J.J. Harper, a young Manitoba Native leader, was mistaken for a car thief and shot during questioning by a Winnipeg police constable on March 7, 1988 in Winnipeg. In the subsequent investigation, the constable was cleared of any wrongdoing. Harper's brother refused to accept the official story and pushed for an investigation into a police cover-up. The chief witness for the Winnipeg police committed suicide before the investigation was concluded. When Annharte wrote this poem, there was little written on the subject. Since then both a book and a film have appeared: *The JJ Harper Story*, written by Winnipeg Free Press Journalist, Gordon Sinclair, Jr. and *Cowboys and Indians: The Killing of J.J. Harper* (which is based on Sinclair's novel), directed by Norma Bailey.

Annharte: Yes. People might say that obviously there was no anal rape or anything like that of J.J. Harper by that particular police officer, but it could appear that way to a Native person who was powerless when a priest or other authority figure did something to them. All the violence fuses into one moment, this particular predator may embody all those things at once. It's part of the brutality on the streets. When someone is terrorizing another person, this is how he would threaten them: "Now I have you in my clutches I can do anything I want with you, I can make fun of you, I can torture you."

Pauline: For sure the sexual abuse that you describe in the poem shows brutality and a flaunting of power. To change to a more positive note: I know you're suspicious of the word "healing," but would it be fair to say that writing poetry can be a healing process for you?

Annharte: Well, certainly healing in the sense of being able to contain something for a while, give it a voice, and therefore face your fears about it. When you're thinking of things—pain or some other thing that may have happened to you—if it just lopes in and out of your brain whenever it feels like it, you're subject to its control; its setting a mood for you. Once you begin to voice your reaction to it, or start to have a dialogue with that pain, you're in a much better place, even to be able to say, "Well, I think I've cried enough over that," or "I think I've learned from that." You can give it more closure.

Pauline: It's a long process?

Annharte: Yes, with each book that I wrote I was exploring more. In the first one, I became aware of all the things I didn't even mention. The silences intrigued me. I got to some of them in *Coyote Columbus Cafe* but definitely in this one I see more of an attempt to go to some of those places and give them more voice than I had done before.

Pauline: One topic that you broach in this book, perhaps for the first time, is hybridity. In "I Want to Dance Wild Indian Black Face" you say "I want to wear a turkey feather in my hair and join the tribe of the / Creole Wild West. I don't want to be authentic all the time" (85).

Annharte: Yes, I wanted to experience freedom from "Indian" identity. Like I say at the end, "I want an Indian day off" (85).

Pauline: As well as resisting that imposed identity, I wonder if this has to do with your own experience as a mixed race person because in terms of bloodlines you aren't in a sense "authentic" because you aren't one hundred percent Indian.

Annharte: Yes, but the funny thing is that even a person who is full blood is not always one hundred percent Indian because they can have a terribly colonized mind. The racial identity doesn't always fit with the cultural identity.

Pauline: Has hybridity been an important issue for you?

Annharte: Well yes, it's a painful thing. You're always made to feel like you're somehow inadequate. You're considered inauthentic. Somehow the racial thing is supposed to give validity to who you are. From day one, if you're not one hundred percent identified with one particular group, you're inadequate. But I've often felt there was a kind of freedom connected to that. At other times, I've felt connected to people of the world of mixed heritage or dual heritage. But I was born with a blue spot on my bum, which is considered a marker for Native babies. For some people that's very important.

Pauline: That makes you authentic! Because your father was white did that mean you grew up in white community?

Annharte: Yes and no. I grew up in a working class area of Winnipeg and not that many Indian people lived in town at that time. But I spent a lot of time with my grandparents. I went to visit them, I spent summers with them, so I was exposed to what that life was like. I went berry-picking with them and so on. Those are some of my fondest memories. It's different from being in a slum in Winnipeg. That memory blurs like the old wallpaper.

Pauline: Were you identified as a Native person at school?

Annharte: Definitely, right away. A lot of people were in fact mixed race but there was no way then to identify people that way. There was no permission for people to identify that way, although people talked about it behind people's back. I remember the Japanese and Germans really getting it, I guess because of the war, but First Nations people were getting it all the time, as an insult.

Pauline: Another topic that you explore in all your books is gender inequality. In this book, in "Squaw Pussy," you create a very positive image.

Annharte: Oh yes, that is positive alright: that's the whole exploration of the continent credited to First Nations women as opposed to the settlers or the explorers.

Pauline: I especially liked this poem because it has such a hip, contemporary cast of women characters, the *"Jaguar woman in black Jaguar car,"* *"Our Cinderella born Native"* and *"Our First Nations business woman"* (72–73).

Annharte: I guess I was questioning the feminist assumptions about women moving up the ladder in terms of business and leadership. But I also felt that with First Nations people, in some places the women who were actually prostitutes contributed to the community as well.

Pauline: Sex workers are an important part of any community, aren't they?

Annharte: Yes, but part of the problem of the women who were killed at the pig farm in Coquitlam was that they were being pushed out of their communities and forgotten.* I guess I'm kind of reclaiming history. I was actually thinking of a particular woman in Saskatoon. I couldn't cash a cheque and this woman offered to take me to her bank. When she came to get me she pulled up in a Jaguar. I found it such a hoot to be riding around in a Jaguar. Of course I was also thinking of Hattie Gossett, a poet in New York, who wrote an amazing poem about "colored pussy" and she had a line about squaw pussy being "killer pussy"—in the sense of being really powerful (*Sister No Blues*). I never would have thought of it that way, but when I wrote this poem, I could see that it was actually First Nations people, especially women, who led these explorers around, who supported them in their adventures, and their settling of the continent. Now some explorers are actually attributing the work on their

* Annharte is referring to the disappearance of close to a hundred women (the majority of whom were First Nations) beginning in 1983 from Vancouver's Downtown Eastside. In 2002, Robert Pickton was charged with the murder of some two dozen of these missing women, based on human remains found buried on his pig farm in Coquitlam, B.C. The police were slow to take action in what has become the largest serial killer investigation in Canadian history. Annharte's comment that these were "forgotten women" is corroborated by one commentator who notes that "the difficulty in assembling a case is that these kinds of killers typically prey on strangers, so it becomes much more difficult for police to make the connections required to confirm the presence of a serial killer." www.cbc.ca/news/background/pickton

expeditions to Native people. They're actually naming them, which is quite recent.

Pauline: In "Squaw Pussy" you again take familiar words and phrases and turn them around or play with them to give them new meanings: for example, "forked feminist fables," or "hiss story, more hiss than story," or your pun on the snake and ladders game. Here's the section:

> dispel typical "squaw" image
> Hollywood Indian princesses
> with braids & dowdy looks
> instead upwardly mobile perms
> replace primitive outlooks
> expected in our stealthy climb
> upward the snakey ladder
> each rung writhing tales
> forked feminist fables
> hiss story, more hiss than story
>
> (72)

Pauline: You obviously enjoy playing around with words.

Annharte: Yeah, I guess so. But I also think there are so many imprecise meanings in the English language and that's why you have to play with the words.

Pauline: In "How to Stop Writing About Indians," you ask: "Given enough poison / Indians will die out but who will give us / the secret remedy or cure for bad writing?" (55). What is your cure for bad writing?

Annharte: Well, to me writing is difficult: it's difficult to allow yourself to feel, to feel the rage about genocide for instance that I was talking about before. You have to find a way to write about that, instead of just running off to the bar to anaesthetize yourself like I used to do with those feelings of rage. It's difficult to feel that it's worth writing about, or that art or writing can contain some of that.

Pauline: How do you get to that point?

Annharte: That's a big question! We've already talked about some of the ways. Turning to story—the personal story—is one way, so the anger has a context. Or sometimes it's not a question of what you're saying but of how you're saying it. I've read other poems about people's oppression and they're very linear, starting off small and getting bigger and bigger up to the grand finale. I wander a bit, back and forth, and I kind of like that as a way to diffuse that obvious place that people are going to, which is the tragedy of it all. I guess I'm subverting that linear process somewhat. This book has a lot of very tough-hitting poems. It almost seems like it's obligatory, but then I thought if I felt these things so strongly and this did influence what I wanted to write about, then this is what I have. It's not like I chose it. It comes from real reactions that I had to events around me.

A Conversation on

Cultural
Poetics" WITH JEFF DERKSEN

Interviewed by Pauline Butling & Susan Rudy

VANCOUVER-BASED POET AND CULTURAL CRITIC JEFF DERKSEN WAS born in Murrayville, B.C. in 1958. In the 1970s he attended David Thompson University Centre in Nelson, B.C. where he earned a B.A. in Creative Writing and English (With Distinction) conferred through the University of Victoria. A former editor of *Writing* magazine, he was a founding member of Vancouver's Kootenay School of Writing (KSW) and served as board member at Calgary's Truck Gallery. In the 1990s and early 2000s, Derksen moved between the cities of Vancouver, Calgary, Banff, New York, and Vienna. Among other activities, he completed both an M.A. (1995) and Ph.D. (2000) in English at the University of Calgary; edited the "Disgust & Overdetermination: a poetics issue" of *Open Letter* (1998); lived in Vienna with his partner, conceptual artist Sabine Bitter; and held a Fulbright in New York City to carry out research on "Concentrated Globalism and Local Culture: Vancouver as Cultural Front" at the City University's Graduate Center for Place, Culture and Politics. His articles on art and poetics have appeared in *Poetics Journal, Fuse, West Coast Line, Open Letter* and elsewhere.

He returned to Vancouver in 2003 to take up a position as Assistant Professor of English at Simon Fraser University.

Derksen's publication history as poet and critic is international in scope, linked to the Language poets in the United States and to experimental poetry communities in Canada, most obviously KSW. He has published three books, all with Vancouver's Talon: *Down Time* (1990) includes poetry published in the 1980s in *Motel, Raddle Moon, Verse, West Coast Line,* and *Writing. Dwell* (1993, winner of the Dorothy Livesay Poetry Award), and *Transnational Muscle Cars* (2003) are the first in a trilogy "addressing place, culture and capital" (Talonbooks website). Chapbooks include *Memory Is the Only Thing Holding Me Back* (1984), *Selfish: Something Deep Inside Liberal Cultural Relativism Says "Yes I Can"* (1993), *Until* (1987; rpt. 1989), and *But Could I Make a Living From It* (2000).

His substantial contribution to Canadian cultural studies and North American poetics involves his investigation—in both critical writing and poetry—of "the burden of history carried by language" (Derksen "Sites" 148). As early as *Down Time* his poetry focussed on the "local" as "an intersection of ideology, signification, and subjectivity" (Derksen "Sites" 151): "The differences are known / and fluctuate at half. Each anecdote / is a suburb and allows me / to own my own rake. So what / do you do when you don't / have one?" (*Down Time* 59). Most recently, in "Fixed City & Mobile World" (2002), an article on Ken Lum's "new city art," Derksen argues for an "urban poetics" hitherto repressed by a nationalist "Canadian cultural history [that] has emphasized space and place rather than how daily life is shaped at the city level" (34).

Derksen's own "urban poetics" becomes even more apparent in *Dwell,* where he critiques multiculturalism and the politics of diversity for being in the service of nationalism, making differences cultural "rather than formed by the pressures of history and capitalism" (40): "Did I say 'my own body'?—I meant the socially / constructed space in which my organs dwell" (67). In *Transnational Muscle Cars* he considers why contemporary social space—"this new imperialism"—behaves "so much like a classic muscle car—all brawn and horsepower, but with little braking power and an inability to negotiate curves" (Talonbooks website): "The misery of millionaires / shows it is a classless society. / It's harder to be happy

/ geopolitically / so new restaurants are reviewed / quickly before they close" (*Transnational* 11).

Several anthologies feature poetry by Jeff Derksen, including Wayman and Wharton's *East of Main* (1989); McGann's guest-edited issue of *Verse*, "Postmodern Poetries: an Anthology of Language Poets From North America and the United Kingdom" (1990); Barnholden and Klobucar's *Writing Class: The Kootenay School of Writing Anthology* (1999); and the second edition of Thesen's *The New Long Poem Anthology* (2001). A selection from *Dwell*—"Host Nation, Host Society"—appears in Messerli's *The Gertrude Stein Awards in Innovative American Poetry 1993–94* (1995). New poems appear in Schwartz's "International not Ultranational: New writing from the new New York" issue of the *Literary Review* (2003). See Derksen's innovative website called "My New Idea": http://www.lot.at/mynewidea_com. Very little critical attention has yet been paid to Jeff Derksen's significant body of work. See Wiens' Ph.D. dissertation, "The Kootenay School of Writing: History, Community, Poetics" (2001), Rudy "'& how else can I be here?'" (2003), and Rudy "'But is it Politics?': Jeff Derksen's `Rearticulatory Poetics'" (forthcoming).

—SR

six

Susan Rudy: Jeff, we've been asking people to focus on their relationship to writing communities. But since so little biographical information about you is in print, could you talk first about your earlier history?

Jeff Derksen: Well, as you know, I'm not interested in narratives so much.

Susan: I know, but I'm asking you anyway!

Jeff: Well, how far back?

Susan: When, for example, did you first take a serious interest in reading?

Jeff: Well, that would have been in the library in New Westminster. I can't remember what year it was, but sometime after 1967 and during the boom of Canadian cultural nationalism. All the library books that were written by Canadian authors had a little maple leaf, a red maple leaf on the spine, so I worked my way around the library clockwise reading every title chronologically that had a maple leaf on the spine. So that ensured that I read plenty of mediocre fiction. John Metcalf, people like that. I can still remember that stuff fairly clearly.

Susan: And were you writing then, did you keep a journal?

Jeff: No, I didn't write until I was 19 or something like that. No, my high school was not particularly great. I think the first reading I saw ever was…actually I think it was Earle Birney. I took a poetry course with George Bowering at Simon Fraser University right after high school in 1976 and he had Earle Birney on the reading list. Somehow that impressed me.

Susan: How?

Jeff: Well, he was doing sound poetry and stuff like that, and then I think Gerry Gilbert came into the classes as well. But Bowering was just immensely entertaining in the class in general; it was in one of those big lecture halls.

I can remember reading both the Olsons: Tillie and Charles. And Gertrude Stein—we read "Susie Asado."

Pauline: How many years were you at Simon Fraser?

Jeff: Just one. I didn't like it. I'd had such a crappy high school education that I decided to go to Douglas College because it was also really cheap. And then I took courses at Douglas College, had various jobs: driving, delivery jobs; working in the weed and feed industry spraying people's lawns; carpentry stuff; dealing with lots of toxins; gas station jobs. And I think I started writing then. I can't particularly remember why or when. I ended up taking a creative writing course from Leona Gom. She was really interesting, and actually published some of my stuff in *Event* magazine. That was in 1979, because I remember hearing about it when I phoned home from the Panama airport, where Erin O'Brien and I were staying overnight in order not to buy a hotel room. So 1999 is my twentieth anniversary of publishing in Canada.

Susan: Why did you go to David Thompson University Centre (DTUC)?

Jeff: One summer I was taking a creative writing course at Simon Fraser University—I was also working in a greenhouse— and I saw a poster announcing that Fred Wah, Tom Wayman, and David McFadden were doing a public presentation about DTUC. So I got all excited and drove out to the Burnaby art gallery. But no one except the janitor, who was sweeping up, was in the room. When I asked about three guys giving a talk he said they got tired of waiting and went off to have a beer and a sandwich. But I did get to talk to Wayman. He was so enthusiastic he somehow convinced me that it would be a good thing to come to DTUC.

Pauline: You've mentioned how Gerry Gilbert, Earle Birney and Leona Gom were all Vancouver-based writers. Were you aware of much writing going on when you were at Douglas? Did you know many writers?

Jeff: I didn't know many writers, but I knew about writers, because I would go to the library. At one point I was doing an essay on pictograms and petroglyphs, and took out Fred [Wah]'s *Pictograms* by mistake.

Pauline: By mistake! Because you thought it was a real book?

Jeff: Yes, I thought it was a real book; I thought it was a useful book. And it sufficiently annoyed me to find out what was going on. So I took out TISH 1–19 and started reading that and from there started reading Charles Olson.

Susan: Then you went to DTUC and started taking courses and writing?

Jeff: Yes. I wouldn't say I thought of myself as a writer, but I was writing. Moving there [to Nelson] was really exciting because everybody was writing all the time and talking about their work.

Susan: Who were the other students then?

Jeff: Gary Whitehead, Noel Hudson, Calvin Wharton, Deanna Ferguson, and Angela Hryniuk. Every year there were some different writers but it was quite cohesive. We hung out in lots of bars and every year there was a strike; students rarely crossed the picket line. So we had these exterior pressures that would bring the community together as well.

Pauline: As I recall, when you arrived at DTUC [Butling was an instructor at DTUC at this time] you were quite knowledgeable already about contemporary poetry and poetics. So you must have been reading before you got there. Or did you take courses at Douglas College.

Jeff: Yes, I took Canadian literature courses, although they emphasized novels and short stories. I remember thinking about links with postcolonialism and Latin America and its use of the short story. In Leona [Gom]'s courses we read poetry. Also, people would come to Nelson and do readings.

Susan: And you also took courses with both Pauline and Fred [Wah]?

Jeff: Yes, at DTUC.

Susan: What courses?

Jeff: I can remember most clearly taking something on the experimental Canadian novel with Pauline.

Pauline: And writing courses with Fred?

Jeff: Writing courses with Fred; writing courses with Tom Wayman.

Susan: Who else was at DTUC teaching then?

Jeff: John Newlove, I think.

Pauline: It varied from year to year, because they had writers-in-residence for six-month terms. Audrey Thomas, Clark Blaise and John Newlove were each there for a while.

Jeff: Colin Browne as well. I also remember that the University of Victoria canceled all my classes, all scheduled to be taught by John Newlove.* After they hired Newlove they decided he couldn't teach because he didn't have a degree. So then I had to make a grievance. The University of Victoria ended up flying out Sean Virgo to teach a course every two weeks because they were legally bound to teach a course that I had signed up for.

Pauline: Did you just take creative writing at DTUC?

Jeff: No, I took a combined English-Creative Writing degree during 1981–84. After DTUC closed in May 1984 I moved into the community house in Vancouver my brother and some friends had, just off Commercial Drive. A bunch of other people from DTUC and Nelson moved to Vancouver as well. That's when the Kootenay School of Writing in Vancouver got started.

Pauline: KSW formed first in Nelson right after DTUC closed. Colin Browne was involved because he had a friend who could get the school non-profit status. As soon as Colin and then Tom Wayman went to Vancouver, they immediately started the Vancouver KSW. But how did you get involved in the KSW and why?

Jeff: To me, it was just an extension of what we were already doing. During my last semester at DTUC I just did political organizing. I was also the coordinator of the media centre that Wayman set up to protest the DTUC closure.

---

* Courses at David Thompson University Centre were credited through Selkirk College for the first and second years and through the University of Victoria for the third and fourth years. Two University of Victoria degrees were available at DTUC: the Bachelor of Fine Arts in Creative Writing, Visual Art, Music, and Theatre and the Bachelor of Education.

Pauline: Yes, the government announced the closure in January. The whole semester was spent doing political work. Everybody was involved in protests, a group went to Victoria to stand in front of the parliament buildings, and various publications were produced.

Jeff: We got a lot of attention in the mainstream media; CBC journal came and did a piece. It was an extremely successful campaign, but politics in B.C. being what they are, any sort of effective protest is seen as a self-interest group.

Pauline: Did that particular experience politicize you or had you been politicized before?

Jeff: The situation in Nelson gave me an avenue for praxis as opposed to being theoretically politicized. But growing up in a working-class family and having the world divided antagonistically between management and workers, that's a politicization right there. My dad was in the Canadian Pulp and Paper Worker's Union and my mom worked as a telephone operator for B.C. Tel.

Pauline: Can we return now to the formation of KSW in Vancouver?

Jeff: Since a bunch of us had moved to Vancouver it felt natural to take the School to Vancouver too. Wayman and Colin Browne were quite organized. They found an office to rent for about $225 a month at 1045 West Broadway and Oak. And then the rest of us, having just moved and being used to living so poorly and cheaply, we just went on and off welfare, unemployment insurance and any grants we could raise through KSW. So, we'd shift from being employed to unemployment insurance, you were either the head of a project or you were unemployed.

Pauline: In the essay on your web site* you say that your experience of economic hardship in B.C. really affected your poetics in the 1980s. Could you talk about that?

Jeff: Right now I'm trying to develop a way to think about the relationship between larger social structures and the structure of the text, modes of writing. It's a methodology I'm calling cultural poetics. I realized that what happened in B.C. in the 1980s was a real breaking down of the liberal notion of political representation. The younger politicized writers weren't writing the kind of representative political poems that the Left had been noted for, people like George Stanley in Vancouver or Wayman

* www.lot.at/mynewidea_com/

to a certain extent. They were turning to what was being called non-representational writing, which I now prefer to call hyper-referential writing. There seemed to be a curious correlation between social structures and the structure of a poem that provided a methodology of writing. At the same time, there was the famous crushing budget that the Social Credit Government in Vancouver called a Restraint budget. I recognized an irony in the type of writing some of the people around KSW were doing. They called it a poetry of excess; Bataille and coming out of McCaffery's readings of Bataille: ideas of general economy versus restrictive economy.

SUSAN: Had you been reading Bataille and McCaffery for several years by this time?

JEFF: Yes.

SUSAN: When did you start reading them?

JEFF: I guess the early 1980s.

SUSAN: At DTUC?

JEFF: Yes, and Bahktin in particular was a big influence for me. As were the Russian Formalists. We approached theory as a necessary part of a poetics. We didn't have a sense of it being hierarchically encoded or somehow out of our reach. We were reading things like the "Talks" edition of *Hills* magazine that Bob Perelman edited.* I guess we were influenced by the Language writers; we had this sense that writers needed to be articulate about their poetics. There has always been a really rigorous and competitive bar scene in Vancouver. And during discussions in the bar, you would be called on to defend yourself in some particular way. We were also hanging out with visual artists at the time, so part of it was how to find a common vocabulary for our practice. We would go to openings together, go to readings together, go to artists' and writers' talks together, trying to find a working vocabulary or a working discourse. If you went to the bar and you hadn't read say, Adorno, you weren't going to have a good time sitting drinking with your friends. There was an impulse on this community level to read theory. People also

---

* Includes articles by David Bromige on "Intention & Poetry," Barrett Watten on "Russian Formalism & The Present," Bob Perelman on "The First Person," Michael Davidson on "The Prose of Fact," Fanny Howe on "Justice" and Ron Silliman on "The New Sentence."

shared books and set up lots of different reading groups. One group was the Grinning Rectos of Late Capitalism; another was a woman's group called The Vultures. Vancouver seems to have a great tradition of intellectual work outside of the academy.

Susan: Were you writing *Down Time* around this time?

Jeff: Yes, the stuff in *Down Time* I guess started around 1985. Because we [KSW] held The New Poetics Colloquium as well, which was the first gathering of the Language poets, so-called. That gave us a sense of our community having larger links rather than just being geographically based.

Susan: And who was "us" at this time?

Jeff: Deanna Ferguson, Kevin Davies, and Nancy Shaw...

Pauline: The New Poetics Colloquium was organized by KSW. But that was directly linked with *Writing* magazine wasn't it?

Jeff: Yes, well, Colin Browne* basically organized that colloquium. The next year, we organized Split Shift: A Colloquium on the New Work Writing. To me these two colloquia indicate the two streams or tenets that were going on at KSW. A straightforward approach to politics and writing through representation and narrative on one hand and on the other a more hyper-referential writing that we were somehow trying to do.

Susan: Can you talk a bit more about what you mean by hyper-referential, as opposed to non-representational?

Jeff: Well, I'm using the hyper-referential to counter the non-referential term. My sense of the hyper-referential comes out of poststructuralist linguistics, that somehow the sign is so flooded with meaning that it becomes non-representational at a certain point. That the sign is based in a materialism that would return it to its material base, and then at a more general level that writing was about language itself. So, it was coming out of a poststructuralist frame, although at the time I wouldn't have been able to think of it that way. But in my own writing practice, it seemed too easy to write the kind of small political, representative poems that I'd been writing previously. And it seemed enormously exciting to use the poem as a vehicle for information, and to include tons of information, and to jump around a bit more within its form.

---

* Editor of *Writing* and a member of the KSW collective.

Susan: A phrase on your web site really caught my eye: "the conditions themselves cry out."

Jeff: That's from Marx's *The Eighteenth Brumaire of Louis Bonaparte,* where he's talking about the social conditions that lead to a revolution, so again there's that idea that I've been working on of overdetermination and contradiction. You get a build-up of overdetermined contradictions within capitalism and that leads to change. But I think we're at a moment when the overdetermined contradictions can just exist, and it doesn't lead to any change.

Pauline: They're just tolerated.

Jeff: They're tolerated and—to fall into a bit of a postmodern vocabulary, they're fluid in themselves—so the contradictions are shifting as well. Nobody expects any big change and that makes us more tolerant of contradictions. Being in Vancouver, as a writer, meant we were filled with social information about contradictions, because at that point, the city was literally and antagonistically split between east and west. Main Street was the dividing line. The West side was the bourgeois, yuppy, moneyed section, while the east was the more ethnically-defined, working-class section. You could really see the contradictions taking place in the city. Especially when Expo 1986 [Expo '86, world fair, Vancouver, 1986] accelerated those contradictions and the Expo site took over the Downtown Eastside. Retrospectively, I recognize that it really was a place of heightened contradictions. Here in Calgary, the city tries to cover up its contradictions and deny its place within a global economy, whereas B.C. has always made it very apparent that it wanted to be part of the Pacific Rim, and all those larger international structures.

Pauline: I'm still interested in hearing you talk about the relation between a "Restraint" economics and what you're calling a poetry of excess.

Jeff: I'm not sure about that. I have to be clearer on the poetics of excess. I'm just trying to imagine the relationship between governmental structures, relationships and policies, and then the structuring of a poem and the decisions you make about how to write. Asking how the conditions themselves cry out is a question about how social structures and economic conditions cry out in a formally politicized poetics.

Pauline: Well I think you're on to something that really works. In the 1980s, the ruptures that you and others brought to your poetics were very different from the ones that occurred in the 1960s. Although you were obviously aware of what had happened in the 1960s.

Jeff: In some sense it seemed like it was an affective reaction to social relations in the 1960s. And so you could admire those writers. Through that, ruptures were made, antagonisms were ignited and worked through in some senses, and that's maybe where I felt some parallel going on. I didn't want to replicate the work, but I saw in the methodology something of interest and of value.

Pauline: Was Tom Wayman fairly important to you for bringing in work writing?

Jeff: Well, for foregrounding class in poetry. Also for believing that poetry was an adequate form to use to talk about class and class politics, and also—I wasn't so much interested in this at the time—but how class was used pedagogically in work writing. To get workers to write about their working experiences using this short, handy form, which didn't cost money. Since it doesn't require a high degree of literacy, so it can be used as a literacy tool. We had a workshop on that at the Split Shift conference.

Pauline: Was your first contact with the Language writers through *Writing* magazine?

Jeff: Yes and through Lyn Hejinian's Tuumba [Press] series. It was a series of really nicely produced, letterpress chapbooks that were very affordable—two to four dollars each. Since we were very strapped for money it was a way to get peoples' work for cheap. Proprioception Books, which was owned by Ralph Maud at the time, didn't factor in the American currency differential, so…

Pauline: Ralph's philanthropy!

Jeff: Yes, whether he knew it or not. Not to mention the fact that it was extremely easy to shoplift from the store. So we would share books in that way.

Susan: Were you at Talonbooks around this time too?

Jeff: No, I wasn't. We were all on and off welfare. First of all I got a job at *Vanguard*, a really great arts/cultural magazine.

Nancy Shaw was writing for them. Mina Tortino, a painter, was working for them. Bill Wood, certainly one of the best art critics in Canada right now, was the associate editor. So that was a golden period. Nancy Shaw was working at the Or Gallery and had links with Artspeak gallery, which started through KSW. We did things with The Western Front and the Contemporary Art Gallery. Everybody would go en masse to these openings and then discuss the work afterwards. The writers were writing about art and the artists were regularly going to the readings. People, like Stan Douglas were doing great work at the time. Everyone was reading and just figuring out how to talk about their practice. We [KSW] had this artist-writers talk series that went on for maybe three or four years.

Susan: Was that the most nourishing community for you?

Jeff: That's the most intense community I've ever experienced. In some ways being at the Banff Centre for a ten-week residency in the fall of 1998 got close to it, because you see the same people all the time and you're talking all the time.

Pauline: To what extent do you think the activity of publishing a magazine, organizing courses, organizing readings, is crucial in forming those kinds of energy centres?

Jeff: I think the energy formed because we had access to sites where events could happen. If someone was coming to town and we wanted to have a reading, we could phone the Western Front, Or Gallery, or Artspeak gallery, or we could have it at KSW. We automatically had a place so it was just a matter of somebody making a handbill or posters and then phoning people or letting them know. You knew you could easily get between 25 and 70 people to an event.

Pauline: But you also planned things too. Do you think the process of making decisions about what was going into *Writing* magazine, and who you were going to invite and so on fostered an intense...

Jeff: Well, particularly because we worked as a collective. It wasn't somebody being excited about one writer, and then organizing for them, and then hoping people would come out. We'd have planning meetings regularly over the year, and then make collective decisions about who we were going to bring. In some ways, if you had enough enthusiasm for someone's work then the project would go through with the help of other people. But at the same time, it had to fit into some kind of criteria. If this could happen at UBC, why would we do it? And the same with *Writing* magazine. When I was the editor, I'd often send back what were probably seen as nasty rejection letters saying things like, "You have access to lots of other writing magazines. Why do you want to get published here?" *Writing* was trying to reflect the structures of feeling—to use Raymond Williams' words—of that extended community, which at that point included New York quite closely. We had been making links with people in New York through magazines and the Segue reading series: the Ear Inn reading series.

Susan: Who were you in contact with in New York?

Jeff: Melanie Nielson, who edited *Big Allis* magazine, Andy Levy, and some more established writers, like Bruce Andrews, who we'd met at the New Poetics Colloquium. And Abigail Child, the writer and filmmaker, came as visiting foreign artist-in-residence. Each year we had a visiting foreign artist-in-residence for two weeks. The first person we had was Susan Howe for two weeks, then Charles Bernstein, Lyn Hejinian, Bruce Andrews, and then Abigail Child. They'd come for two weeks, do a reading, a talk, and a weeklong seminar. Some people did workshops; Abigail did a workshop on melodrama and film. Now that I've been in the academy, I can say that it was more like a graduate course, but one where the stakes were higher in a sense.

Pauline: Do you think that kind of intense activity only gets sustained for a certain period of time, and people inevitably turn to other things? Colin Browne got a "regular" job out at Simon Fraser University. You got a job at Talonbooks and later went to graduate school. Wayman got a job.

Jeff: Well KSW expanded but not in Vancouver, although it's been equally intense. And now my more intense connections with a poetics community are in New York. I was just in San Francisco, and I have a sense of what's going on there as well. So it's kind of a collective that is not based in a site. This breaks older tropes of poetics of place, or communities being geographically based. The community expanded. That started with the links we made with New York when people were regularly invited to read down in the Ear Inn's Segue reading series.

Susan: Why did you come to Calgary to go to graduate school, instead of New York?

Jeff: Well I applied to SUNY Buffalo once and I got rejected, and then I applied again and got in. But it's all linked with personal decisions as well. My mother had just died a couple of weeks before. I had to make the decision, and I might have been uneasy about moving to Buffalo or a place I didn't really know; I didn't really know Calgary that well, but at least it felt closer to Vancouver.

Susan: Did you ever have a sense of a community or an intense intellectual context in Calgary.

Jeff: Nothing comparative, because I haven't been able to find or create a link between the writing community and the visual arts community. I think the writing community is fairly self-contained. At this point, I spend more time with people in the visual arts community. I'm on the board of Truck Gallery, which is one of the most exciting artist-run centres right now.

Pauline: Your sense of community since you've come to Calgary has been much more what you call a transnational community hasn't it?

Jeff: For myself yes, because I've been getting asked to do things more in other countries.

Pauline: In one of your recent essays you differentiate between a transparent internationalism and something that is more conscious.

Jeff: One of the influences in how I've come to think about that is Immanuel Wallerstein's idea of geoculture, where you also have antisystemic movements within this geoculture. You can trace this through larger instances, such as the Pan African movement, the assembly of the United Nations, or even through transnational writing structures such as PEN. Or within pop music, those Save the World type things they were doing at a certain point. So I guess I see that transnationalism as having a critical function. It seems limiting to talk about the contradictions and overdeterminations of a world system from within a too localized space. Somehow—maybe I am being too cautious about the local—but it seems that you have to be more within a system that you're going to critique. That is, moving away from an idea of opposition and resistance to an idea of rearticulation. That opposition and resistance has imagined itself as being outside

of the debilitating structures of power, and has been critical
from the exterior, whereas rearticulation is about disarticulating
and rearticulating linkages within systems, somehow rearrange
structures from within. To be critical of a world system, you have
to somehow imagine yourself within it, as opposed to barking at
it from a local position.

Pauline: Doesn't "to articulate" mean to link up, the way the boxcars
in a train are linked for instance?

Jeff: Or like those buses that can bend around corners.

Pauline: Have you commented on this somewhere before?

Jeff: Yes, in a talk I just did in San Francisco called "Poetry and
Social Relations: Recent Rearticulatory Practices." But I'm just
lifting the term from Chantal Mouffe and Ernesto Laclau's idea
of radical democracy.* I'm looking at how Lawrence Grossberg
has used it in terms of cultural studies and moving it into this
field of cultural poetics.

———

Susan: How much has your experience travelling affected your sense
of participating in a global community? Is that participation in
fact based on relationships you forged in person?

Jeff: Not so much, because to me the contradictions within
global capital are totally accentuated at the local level.
One of my poems—"Jerk" or "Jerk Jeff Derksen" on my
website—talks about wanting an art more complicated than
The Gap. The Gap outsources for its labour. They can make
T-shirts more cheaply in Malaysia than in Hong Kong, but
making a shirt with a collar is cheaper in Hong Kong. So if
you went to The Gap and spent a couple of hundred dollars on
looking like a Gap person, then actually you're wearing all the
contradictions of capitalism on your body. Not to fetishize
the body, but you are kind of hauling this stuff around. So it
also happens at an extremely localized level. Althusser makes
the same point when he says that ideology never says, "I am
ideological." I think the world system never says "I am a world
system"; it says "Think locally act locally." Which on one level

---

* See Laclau and Mouffe, *Hegemony and Socialist Strategy: Towards a Radical
Democratic Politics.*

has to happen. But I'm trying to imagine how larger modes of production get worked out on a local level, even if that local level is The Gap store in your mall. Why can people send money to UNICEF, or phone the cerebal palsy association to come and pick up a bag of clothes here in Calgary, for example—be politicized at that level—but at the same time have absolutely no problem wearing a pair of Nikes if they know the person who made the Nikes probably gets paid a nickel a day? Those contradictions within world capitalism get worked out at a local level. In my more recent poetry I'm trying to heighten the contradictions of global capital within poetry. Poetry is an effective form for that heightening because of the rapid semantic shifts that first started around ideas of voice. My inheritance—through the Language poets—of the Bahktinian sense of heteroglossia and dialogic relationships hasn't made me arrive at the poem as a vehicle for being able to put these contradictions side-by-side. I try to work at the level of the sentence as opposed to sentence-by-sentence following that model.

Pauline: So the column-by-column movement in "Jerk" (website) isn't setting up some kind of binary?

Jeff: No. I did "Jobber" and "Until" on my website in the sliding columns because "Until" was published in *Down Time* (11–22). And then I did the conversation with Louis Cabri. One day I started extending "Until" and this poem called "Jobber." And I realized they'd never be published side-by-side. In this instance the technology of the web would actually allow these two things to co-exist. You can slide them up and down and read them at different points. It just seemed one way of publishing on the web that actually suited what I was trying to do.

Susan: How do you see the relationship between your early work and writing experiences and the theoretical work you read later?

Jeff: Well I never saw theory as being separate from life. Actually Dorothy Trujillo Lusk said something interesting a while ago. We were talking on the phone about how Gramsci was never read as someone who was highly theoretical. He was seen as a cultural theorist who had things to say about the society we live in. When we move him out of his context, then he gets read as somehow being theoretical and difficult instead of being practical and theoretical. In the same way, I didn't know that Bahktin was

supposed to be difficult and highly theoretical. I approached
his work as a practical thing that I had to know in order to be
a writer. I always took a practical stand towards language as a
material. I thought you had to know language as a material, in
the same way that if you were a carpenter, you had to know nails
and wood.

———

Susan: Did your move to Calgary to do graduate work in the 1990s
affect your writing?
Jeff: In some ways; being at the University clarified what I'm doing
with my writing because what I do as an academic feels quite
separate from what I do as a writer.
Susan: So, although you've resisted splitting your critical from
your so-called "creative" work, you felt you needed to maintain
the distinction here?
Jeff: Yes. I see the academy as both an enabling site and a site to be
resisted, or rather rearticulated. But it's workplace politics as well,
trying to rearticulate the site you're working in. At the same time
there doesn't seem to be as intense or as rigorous a theoretical
debate going on in the academy as I find within my poetic
communities. So I'm not sure exactly what the effect of being in
the academy has been. It gives you access to other sites, and that
was one reason why I knew at the beginning that I wanted to
move into the academy. I also wanted to test out the knowledge I'd
gained in this other community and see how it worked alongside
the kind of knowledge gained in graduate school.
Pauline: Why did you not do a degree in creative writing?
Jeff: You mean why did I do a critical degree? Because writing
was something I was already doing and I had a really exciting
structure in place, so I didn't need to either add to it or replace it.
I didn't have as much access to a critical writing community or
even as much access to journals, etc. I wanted to test my critical
knowledge but I didn't want to bring my writing practice into
too narrow a structure. The idea of having to select a supervisory
committee within a university so I could talk about my poetry
was not appealing to me. It may sound arrogant, but I felt that
unless those people had done the work that I had done within
my poetic community, I didn't want to be explaining to them

what I was up to. I wanted the university to offer me something I didn't have, rather than try and duplicate something I already had access to.

Susan: Do you see an intellectual relationship between your critical projects—the Fulbright research you're about to undertake for example—and your writing? Or are they quite separate activities?

Jeff: In some ways they are separate. But I think of the Fulbright project (a comparative study of Canadian and American multicultural poetry, policy, and initiatives) as useful in the sense that it got me excited about reading Charles Olson again. I've been reading *The Maximus Poems* as an articulation or a formation of foreign policy for a nation, as opposed to a defining of the local. So I was thinking of critical writing as having an effect on policy.

Pauline: You've been fairly critical of nationalism—for good reason. But your title *Dwell* implies that you want to emphasize locatedness.

Jeff: Well, yes, but "to dwell" also means, "to worry," right? In the sense of "dwelling" on something. I guess I don't think of dwell so much now. Instead I've been thinking about circulation. It makes sense since I'm moving around more. But I'm also interested in how language and information circulate, and even how social structures circulate. In *Dwell* I think I was sometimes falling into a common but problematic ethnographic trope where you travel to another country and then you find out more about yourself than what you find there. Self-awareness isn't enough. Unfortunately for Marx.

Susan: I was just thinking of another field of meaning for the word "dwell" that is suggested by the phrase "don't dwell on it" meaning don't examine something too closely or look at the implications. I've always read the title—*Dwell*—as being directed at the reader who is commanded by the imperative form to DWELL! For me, the title requires that I occupy the complexity of what's going on at every moment. In fact, that's one of the most intriguing aspects of your work for me.

Jeff: I like reading poetry fast. I read it as fast as I can, but I read it over and over and over.

Pauline: Is your anti-nationalism connected to the strong links you've made with U.S. writers?

Jeff: I think it emerged out of a shared politics. But the shared politics has been one that's shifted. In some ways, it was feeling an emergent generation or an emergent community of writers, who were coming out of the space created by the Language poets, and sharing sites of publication with the magazines. KSW could set up readings in these various sites. Segue reading series at the Ear Inn had a site. So we just started making links in that we were organizing in similar ways, and we were approaching poetry and poetics as a public project.

Pauline: Did you find sites of connection elsewhere in Canada?

Jeff: To some extent in the work that Louis Cabri and Rob Manerry were doing in Ottawa [Transparency Machine/*hole* magazine]. And I had a few weaker links with Toronto. Recently I've been in contact with Darren Wershler-Henry, Christian Bök, especially Peter Jaeger, who has gone international as well. He's in London right now.

Susan: What projects do you have planned for the next few years?

Jeff: I'll probably be in Brooklyn, splitting my time between New York and Vienna because I fell in love and got a Fulbright! To be more specific, I'm examining a global system through a performative poetics. I'll be working on the comparative study I've mentioned and finishing a new manuscript of poetry called "All Mod Contradictions" [retitled *Transnational Muscle Cars*].

Susan: To what does the word "mod" refer?

Jeff: It's from The Jam album *All Mod Cons* (Weller's finest moment). I'm merging The Jam, the late punk band from Britain, with Louis Althusser, using his essay on contradiction. So "All Mod Contradictions." Again I'm returning to the sense that the conditions themselves cry out, and to the tensions within global capitalism.

Pauline: What conditions do you think are crying out now?

Jeff: To contradict what I said a little earlier, they cry out differently, and it depends on where you're looking at them from.

Pauline: How do you see them from where you are here in Calgary?

Jeff: The largest contradiction I can see in Calgary—one I'm no longer interested in pursuing—involves the covering up of contradictions.

Susan: Does that mean they don't cry out?

Jeff: They cry out more loudly for some people. For the working class they cry out quite loudly here. This city has quite a functional split—doesn't Calgary have the largest gap between rich and poor in any city in Canada? Yet it imagines itself as this happy, friendly place where we all like the same things. So how those contradictions are covered up seems to be the biggest contradiction. Living here I've become interested in how social space has been managed in order for those contradictions not to show. There are no real clusters of different ethnic and racialized groups as there are in other cities, so the conditions aren't so visible.

Pauline: Except in the northeast, but it's very much a site where nobody else goes.

Jeff: Still, it's very dispersed and you do have these major roads that run through, the trails that effectively split up the city. They cut right through any social space that would allow things to happen. I have one line in a new poem, "there is space / but I can't say / that it's social" ("Nobody Like You" *Transnational* 42). Calgary has been imagined as a city for upper middle class people to drive around in comfortably. It didn't really imagine that people would live or work here. It just imagined the managers of the people driving around who would need good places to park and lots of highways.

Pauline: So Calgary is a site that's in need of disarticulating, in order for some of those contradictions to become more visible.

Susan: Can you talk about how you—or Marx for that matter— understand the concept of "the conditions themselves"? Do we need to know, for example, how those conditions are linked to actual bodies? Who cries when the conditions themselves cry out?

Jeff: Well, this returns us to the idea that within capitalism there's an inherent flaw that can make it blow apart. That's the contradiction I'm interested in. The flaws are there, but it manages to hold together.

Susan: Do you see yourself as enabling the conditions, as they cry out, to be heard?

Jeff: Well, I'd say that I'm determined by them. But then I would also give myself some performative role as an agent. Or indicate agency by revealing the contradictions. That's the first step towards rearticulation.

Susan: Revealing them to whom?

Jeff: Well revealing them to whatever audience you have, however culture circulates within whatever markets it has access to. To me it always seems like an act of faith. You can be pessimistic about that or you can be optimistic, because I've seen how people's poetics have made decisions in their lives and how those have effects. For example, I wouldn't have moved to Vancouver to be on welfare if I didn't have a belief in the poetics I was talking about. I'm not saying it's about living your poetics. But you make decisions that determine how things are going to unfold. Very basically, I'm going to do volunteer work for a cultural group as opposed to I'm going to get my career on track, that kind of thing.

Pauline: I don't know if I want to ask this question of an anxious male generation, but to what extent is gender an issue for you?

Susan: That's partly my question too, I mean whose conditions are you interested in?

Jeff: I think in *Dwell* I was trying to show gender as a construction, and maybe at some points as performative, but also as one that is determined socially and has social effects.

Susan: And real conditions.

Pauline: Can we talk about the poems a bit more specifically? I'm interested in taking your notion of disarticulation a little further. "Neighbourhood" (*Dwell* 50–59), for example, is not necessarily that "difficult," but each line tends to hang on its own:

> does seam meander
> redundant anthropologist stigma
> matters erst stinger
> reverse severance cents (50)

Jeff: "Neighbourhood" in the title is mimetic in the sense that each word has to start with at least two of the previous word's ending letters. Those ending letters are then transposed. It starts with the word "Neighbourhood" itself and then I move to "does seam meander." Other lines are "david did idle lentils" (57), which seems like a sentence. I made up that arbitrary rule because I was writing while working at Talonbooks. I always liked being in the middle of a poem. I'd have the file open and I could just go into it and then add a couple of words by just looking at the previous word and having flipped those letters around and then somehow make a link. So it was a way of proceeding through the poem. Then I put the square brackets (in the Vancouver tradition of using square brackets, like Kevin Davies' *Pause Button*) as kind of an authorial intrusion into the poem:

> derived decant anthro [my experience
> of leisure] revived death (56)

Or in this section:

> david did idle lentils
> slug luggage gage
> genuflect ectomorph physical [more 1970s
> for me] meal lame me (57)

Because I was a copyeditor and a proofreader I use all the punctuation in the standard forms. So the square bracket is the authorial or editorial intrusion into a text.

Pauline: But is the effect of the different methods that you've used to disarticulate or open up the meaning and let it float there? How are you working toward rearticulation?

Jeff: I was thinking more of "Neighbourhood" as having a function within the book, which was to not have one dominant aspect of language hold on too long. Thinking of Roman Jakobson's idea of a dominant, I wanted to emphasize that the functions of language always circulate. One will be a dominant at one particular point, so whenever the semantic was the dominant then I'd flip to make the morphological dominant. And that's what "Neighbourhood" is doing, using language as a material to move away from the semantic. So it has a function within the book rather than being a project on its own.

Pauline: In the 1960s the tone leading of vowels was supposed to lead you into revelations of the unconscious. But I sense a very different process here for you.

Jeff: Well maybe I fall into being a mystic Marxist in some sense, in that the revelation will have to be ideology revealed.

Susan: Are you reading the words you choose to inscribe as you're moving the letters around? Thinking of all the words that come up with "nd" or whatever, are you making the choice about which word to put down? Is that where your ideological layers come in?

Jeff: I was also trying to write about the news of the day in that poem; I was trying to talk about things that were going on at the same time in Vancouver, where I largely wrote that. How can I dampen the semantic through this formal method, yet maintain a relationship to larger social structures?

Pauline: Can we look at the series, also in *Dwell*, called "Hold On To Your Bag Betty" (32–45)? There are six sections, each called "Excursives." That's a very curious term, excursive.

Jeff: Oh, I took the words "excursion" and "discursive"...

Pauline: And you put them together. Why?

Jeff: I was trying to write a self-conscious ethnographic text. I'd been working, as an editor, through the Museum of Anthropology at UBC, so I had been reading new anthropological stuff like James Clifford and Mary Louise Pratt and Talal Asad. So I was interested in moving that methodology into a poetics and then using the sentence as the unit of construction within that: new sentence meets new ethnographic methodology. And then because I'd got a Canada Council grant, Erin [O'Brien] and I decided to go to Spain with the money. It was in 1992, so it seemed kind of this funny reverse journey of the ironic celebrations of the quincentenary of the discovery of America. We wanted to see how Spain and Portugal were imagining themselves at that time.

Pauline: There's often a very ironic "I" though in this series...

Jeff: Yes, I was trying to get away from an authorial, ethnographic subject. Yes, I was being ironic. The irony is that you go somewhere and you learn about the self, as opposed to going somewhere and becoming aware of the place. So I think that text makes me a little nervous because it vacillates between that self-awareness, ironizing that self, and then also the irritable reaching after the comprehension of the other in some sense. But those are all traps of ethnographic tropes.

Pauline: Steve McCaffery comments that "the demise of the phenomenological voice is what these poems provide us with."

Jeff: Well, it comes back in "Hold On To Your Bag Betty."

Pauline: Does McCaffery's comment make sense to you?

Jeff: Well contextually it does. It was written in 1990 or something like that when there was a struggle going on between writing communities—the refigured subject that Language poets and post-language writing were trying to construct, and the more self-assured or stable phenomenological subject, the unified or stable subject.

Pauline: Is "the phenomenological self" unified and stable? I wonder if he was referring to voiced poetry.

Jeff: Yes, I think so. The tension is between a poetics of speech and what's supposed to be the great rupture that initiates the Language poets, the "I hate speech" ("On Speech") essay by Robert Grenier. But one of most stable, phenomenological subjects I can think of is Ron Silliman in his big project, *Alphabet.* So this question was worked out antagonistically in a discourse of poetics, but not so in the poetry.

Pauline: One of the things I like about *Dwell* is the way you do take on the self in various ways, rather than just pretending you can get rid of it. A lot of writing pretends to but never does get rid of the self, so it's better to work with it more deliberately.

Jeff: That might have come out of *Down Time*—trying to write a working-class self or a working-class subject, or the subject that's determined by the conditions of the working class.

Susan: Or your ironic distance from that.

Jeff: Yes, which is also another position within the working class. There's nothing more classical about the working class than trying to get the hell out of the working class.

Pauline: In *Down Time* did you work with class issues?

Jeff: They are very much on the surface in Vancouver. You're living them and the tensions of them every day. Not having a stable income or much money at all, any kind of change to your environment initiated by the "dominant class" would send you scurrying. When Expo came to town, we all thought for sure we were going to lose our apartments and end up living in the suburbs of Burnaby in someone's basement suite, the most horrifying thing we could possibly think of. So I was in some ways trying to use the vocabulary that I grew up with, that I was comfortable with, and bring it into this different social atmosphere, and also into a community that doesn't normally use that discourse, or that vocabulary. Although that was the really exciting thing about KSW. A lot of the vocabulary at KSW, especially in Deanna Ferguson's work and Dorothy Trujillo Lusk's in particular, was really a working-class language. We'd read in bars and clubs and stuff, and I can remember people coming up to me and saying how much they recognized that vocabulary. These were people who don't want anything to do with poetry, although they'll recognize a particular vocabulary.

Pauline: What's the connection between your class politics and the difficulty or impenetrability of some of your writing?

Jeff: In another essay, I talk about the organic link, using that term from Gramsci, the idea of organic intellectuals who remain true to their class. You can be working class and intellectual at the same time; you're not making a split. That organic link between intellectuals and their community was exactly the aspect of the social sphere that was broken by the Social Credit government. The unions used to have dinners and things. I remember going to Wobbly dinners, International Workers of the World dinners, in Vancouver, where there'd be poetry readings and someone like Utah Philips would play and sing and stuff like that. And Wayman would be serving up the dinner. That kind of organic connection between the working class and an intellectual working class was broken at that time, very consciously smashed, by that government. People at KSW inherit or move into this social sphere that's been radically altered, and that's why they're thinking about radically changing the methodology of writing. If representational politics obviously doesn't work, when 60,000 people are called a special interest group, what's the sense of writing poems that represent people's lives in some sense? We're moving towards not a mimetic relationship with social relations, but maybe an antagonistic one that sets you up in an antagonistic relationship with the previous poetics in a sense, one that was representational. And that's why I always felt closer links to the TISH group. How come they were never called so-called TISH group, like the Language poets? I always felt closer to them.

Pauline: Because they were more "shitty"?

Jeff: Yes, the so-called shit anagram. Yes, I felt closer to them than someone like Brian Fawcett, who had a lot of confidence in his phenomenological subject, and also in his poetry as an iterative act—like Ginsberg with his "I hereby declare the Vietnam war over." Well, go ahead and declare it over, but.... In that talk that I had with Silliman,* I ended up emphasizing the contingent and tactical over the strategic, and that seemed to upset him quite a bit, that having a quicker response to things somehow wasn't giving up on a longer term project. I see extra textual rearticulations as a method to move texts or moments into a related problematic or field in order to read the effects of a text or formation, a methodological "making it new" perhaps.

* See Derksen and Silliman, Phillytalks #3.

seven Hybridity*and* Asianicity

IN CANADA

Interviewed by Susan Rudy

Fred Wah is a poet, editor, teacher, and critic who moved to Vancouver in 2003 after his retirement from the University of Calgary where he taught for 14 years. Born in 1939 in Swift Current, Saskatchewan to a Swedish mother and a father of both Chinese and English ancestry, he spent most of his childhood in Nelson, British Columbia (1948–58). Wah completed a B.A. in Music and English at the University of British Columbia (1958–62) and was one of the founding editors of TISH: *A Poetry Newsletter, Vancouver* (1961–63). While at UBC, he studied literature with Warren Tallman, creative writing with Robert Creeley, and attended Charles Olson's seminar at the 1963 UBC Summer Poetry Workshop.

In 1963–64, Wah studied with Robert Creeley at the University of New Mexico where Wah did graduate work and founded *Sum* magazine. In 1964, he moved to Buffalo where he studied poetics with Charles Olson (1964–65) and linguistics with Henry Lee Smith Jr. (1965–67) at the State University of New York (M.A. 1967). In Buffalo, Wah became a contributing editor to the *Niagara*

Frontier Review and *The Magazine of Further Studies* and a contributing editor to *Open Letter* magazine, founded by Frank Davey in Canada in 1964. In 1967, Wah returned to the Nelson area of British Columbia to teach at the Castlegar campus of Selkirk College (1967–78; 1985–89) and at David Thomson University Centre (1978–84) where he was the founder (1978) and Director (1978–82) of the DTUC Writing program. Wah was also one of the founders of the Kootenay School of Writing in Nelson, following the closure of DTUC in 1984. While living in the Nelson area, Wah's editing work continued with *Scree* magazine, *Open Letter* (1964 – present), *Net Work: Selected Writing by Daphne Marlatt* (ed. Wah 1980), and as contributing editor (with Frank Davey) of *Swift Current*, Canada's first electronic newsletter.

With Wah's first book of poetry, *Lardeau* (1965), Wah began a life-long exploration of an improvisational, disjunctive poetics based partially on his interest in jazz. His early books were also insistently located within a personal geography and history: *Mountain* (1967), *Among* (1972), *Tree* (1972), *Earth* (1974), and *Pictograms from the Interior of B.C.* (1975). This phase of Wah's poetics culminate with *Loki Is Buried at Smoky Creek: Selected Poems* (1980). In the 1980s, Wah emerged as a central figure in the articulation of a racialized poetics in North America with *Breathin' My Name with a Sigh* (1981), *Waiting For Saskatchewan* (1985), winner of the Governor General's Award for Poetry, and more recently, with his "verse biotext about racial anger," *Diamond Grill* (1996), winner of Alberta's Howard O'Hagan Award for Short Fiction.

Wah's poetry has continued to be linguistically adventurous, formally innovative, and conceptually challenging, especially in an on-going series titled "MHT" or "Music at the Heart of Thinking" that began with *Music at the Heart of Thinking* (1987) and in subsequent poetry collections *So Far* (1991) and *Alley Alley Home Free* (1992, which won Alberta's Stephansson Award for Poetry). His essay collection, *Faking It: Poetics and Hybridity* (2000, awarded the Gabrielle Roy Prize for Literary Criticism in English), elaborates his life-long interest in both poetics and hybridity. In the 1990s, Wah also completed several collaborative projects with visual artists, including *articulations* with Calgary artist Bev Tosh, *High Tea* a performance with Vancouver-based Haruko Okano, and "Lullabye [xi] and Sea," a catalogue essay on the work of Vancouver photographer Marian Penner Bancroft. Wah has served as writer-in-residence at the Universities of Manitoba (1982–83) and Alberta (1988–89), has taught numerous writing workshops, has served on the Racial Minorities and Social Justice Committees of The Writers' Union of Canada (TWUC) and as its President in 2001–2002. His work has been anthologized in *The New Long Poem Anthology* (Thesen 1991, 2001), *Premonitions: The Kaya Anthology of New Asian North American Poetry* (Lew 1995), *Making a Difference: Canadian Multicultural Literature* (Kamboureli 1996), *Uncommon Wealth: An Anthology of Poetry in English* (Besner et al. 1997), 15 *Canadian Poets x* 3 (Geddes 4th edition 2001), and *A New Anthology of Canadian Literature in English* (Bennett and Brown 2002).

Critical attention has been steadily increasing since Derksen's "Making Race Opaque: Fred Wah's Poetics of Opposition and Differentiation" (1995) appeared. See Banting, *Body, Inc.* (1995); Diehl-Jones, *Fred Wah and His Works* (1997); Saul, "Displacement and self-representation: theorizing contemporary Canadian biotexts" (2001); Sugars "'The negative capability of camouflage': fleeing diaspora in Fred Wah's *Diamond Grill*" (2001); McGonegal, "Hyphenating the Hybrid 'I': (Re)Visions of Racial Mixedness in Fred Wah's *Diamond Grill*" (2002); Kamboureli, "Faking It: Fred Wah and the Postcolonial Imaginary" (2003); Budde, "After postcolonialism: migrant lines and the politics of form in Fred Wah, M. Nourbese Philip, and Roy Miki" (2003); and Davey et al., "Fred Wah: Alley Alley Home Free," a special issue of *Open Letter* (2004) featuring contributions from the Poetry Conference and Festival for Pauline Butling and Fred Wah at the University of Calgary, May 15–18, 2003.

—SR

seven

Susan Rudy: Would you tell me about the process of writing *Diamond Grill*?

Fred Wah: *Diamond Grill* started as a run I took at the three-day novel contest on Labour Day weekend in 1988. bp[Nichol] had been encouraging me to try prose because he felt that writers should try all kinds of writing. I'd always been intimidated by prose but I decided to try it. I didn't get that much written, about 60–80 pages of stuff in three days. I just let it go and told very simplistic anecdotes. It certainly wasn't a novel. I had no structure in mind and what was driving it was still what had been driving *Breathin' My Name With a Sigh* and *Waiting for Saskatchewan*: the notion of my father, the push to try to say something about myself. Looking back, I see that I was getting caught up in questions of identity that I hadn't really had any means to think about before.

Susan: Questions of identity were not overt for you as you worked on *Breathin' My Name With a Sigh*? Did you have any consciousness then of the complexity of your identity?

Fred: Well, yes, I was aware of it then. The bio starts for me with a poem I wrote in *Pictograms from the Interior of B.C.* in which I mention my cousins.* That poem became provocative for me because I kept wondering, how did that get in there? Why all of a sudden "cousins"? And then a combination of other poems about death, about our dog dying, just sort of accumulated to a point where I started addressing my father. But to go back to the writing of *Diamond Grill*, all I really wanted to do, or felt that I could do, was simply start telling stories about growing up in a cafe as a way to try to nail down the father a little more. I had this incredible vacuum in my life because my father died when he was so young, only 54. That was in 1966 and I was in Buffalo at graduate school. I hadn't really spent much time with him since I left Nelson in 1957. Besides, he was a very hard-working man so I never spent that much time with him anyway, although we did have family times together. When this all tumbled down on me in the late 1970s, there was this big hole in me that I just fell into. But what permitted me to start writing about the father or about race and identity was something going on in the late 1970s both for myself as a person, as a poet, as a writer, as well as something going on in the culture more generally. The Japanese Redress movement started then for example. All of a sudden a dialogue about Asianicity in Canada was possible. If you think back in terms of a literary milieu around the late 1960s and early 1970s, documentary poems were beginning to be written based on ethnicity, lots of poems with family photographs, the prairies—like Andrew Suknaski's *Wood Mountain Poems*. In B.C. and the prairies, there was an opening up to oral history. Look at Daphne [Marlatt] doing *Steveston*, and the Hastings Street book [*Opening Doors*]. One of my favourite publications

---

* September spawn
fish weirs everywhere
all through the narrows.

Upstream, upstream.

A feast for all of us
cousins and old friends
everybody dancing
like crazy, eh? (16)

around that time was a B.C. oral history magazine [*Sound Heritage*]. Daphne had done some work as an oral historian for the B.C. archives. Suddenly story became possible. And B.C. history. Craig Andrews (an historian) and I did a course called "The B.C. Story" at Selkirk College. He did the history and I did the literature. And during that course we brought in Roy Miki and several other Japanese Canadians from Vancouver. We started talking about the Japanese Canadian history in B.C. and later on Joy Kogawa's book *Obasan* came out in 1981. All of a sudden there was an opening for questions of historical identity, like "where did you come from," that up until then had been possible only in a very silenced and unproblematic way. The fact that I was partly Chinese—George Bowering, for example, would know that and would kid around about it maybe—but it was never an ingredient in any of our discourse around poetry and poetics. Race and ethnicity were not part of language, period. I guess you can trace it back to the bilingual and multicultural legislation at the time.* All of a sudden the term multiculturalism starts coming up and you start thinking, here we are. What is this place? In the 1950s and early 1960s those questions weren't asked at all.

Susan: So you suddenly had permission to tell your personal history? Why then did you move into poetry with that material?

Fred: Well, I wasn't a storyteller. I wasn't a prose writer and I had always been suspicious of story because story is something that had been very much controlled by the "mainstream," by the West, a British inheritance. I had been able to undermine that for myself in poetry because poetry is language-based, whereas story is much more context-based. Daphne was very interested

---

* The Royal Commission on Bilingualism and Biculturalism (1963–71) was chaired by André Laurendeau (then editor in chief of *Le Devoir*, who had suggested a Royal Commission to examine Quebec's dissatisfaction), A. Davidson Dunton and, after Laurendeau's death in 1968, Jean-Louis Gagnon. Formed to "examine existing bilingualism and biculturalism, and to recommend ways of ensuring wider recognition for the basic cultural dualism of Canada" (Laing, *Canadian Encyclopedia*), the Commission recommended The Official Languages Act (1969), a federal statute that was passed, declaring French and English to be Canada's official languages. The term "multiculturalism" began to be used in the 1960s to counter the term "biculturalism," the term popularized by the Royal Commission. "Multiculturalism" also refers to a government policy proclaimed in 1971.

in prose and story and she started a magazine, *periodics: a magazine of innovative prose*, and Bowering was writing a lot of story. But I just didn't get into it.

Susan: Do you see *Diamond Grill* as a series of stories?

Fred: Oh yes. *Diamond Grill* was a problem for me because I had sixty or seventy pages of anecdotes and short things and fragments but I didn't know what to do with it. I'd fiddle around with it once in a while and put it away and not be very satisfied. From 1988–94, I was paying more attention to the ongoing series "Music at the Heart of Thinking" as a compositional activity. But I guess the one thing that opened up writing prose for me was the prose poem, the utaniki *Grasp the Sparrow's Tail*, which I wrote in the early 1980s when we were in Japan. I can remember sitting in our apartment in Kyoto one morning. I was writing on this big old typewriter because we didn't have computers in those days to carry around the world. I was trying to rewrite and rewrite and rewrite (you could spend a whole day re-typing) a piece that used the second person "you." But I was getting tired of talking to my father as "you" so I just turned it and started using it as a reflexive "you" and then mixing it up. I thought, "Oh, this is interesting." All I need to do is twist this a little bit. So it was the second person that really opened up prose for me. I got interested in the fact that one could interpellate, one could call oneself.

Susan: Were you also interested in the ambivalence of that address? That when you write "you" the referent could be you, or your father, or both?

Fred: Well, it also foregrounded questions of identity for me. In the early 1980s I didn't quite know how to figure out if "I" am really this split subject. Who is speaking and who's being spoken? So I had the material from the three-day novel contest and I had done some of the prose poems in *Waiting for Saskatchewan* (the "Elite" series pronounced "ee-light") and I just let the prose go.

Susan: Is *Diamond Grill* "prose poetry"?

Fred: Some of it is and some of it isn't. Some of it is just purely descriptive. It's a balancing act. I think Aritha [van Herk] as the editor had to make some decisions, or suggestions, as to which way to go sometimes. I would be quite happy to blow things up and just let them trickle off into the cryptic, but narrative won't let you do that too much. Having done the three-day novel contest I realized you could just tell a very quick story, you don't have to write a big story. Life isn't a big story; life is very photographic. I was also working with photographs I got from my mother as source material.

Susan: Breathin' My Name With a Sigh includes a number of "mother poems" as well as "father poems." And the poems addressed to the father are much closer to narrative, addressing that "you." The mother poems are more cryptic, more lyrical in a funny way, more disjointed. Why and how did you move toward such a concentration on your paternal history?

Fred: Good question. I guess it's something I haven't figured out yet. That question has bothered me. I've thought about it. In *Waiting for Saskatchewan* I decided to try to open up the mother content as well as stop this father content from taking over so much. In "This Dendrite Map: Father/Mother Haibun" series (73–96) I tried to bring in the mother. I was feeling guilty that I hadn't addressed her, that it was such a father narrative. My feminism made me feel that my mother must have influenced me too. I don't think that poem works, quite. It seems fairly constructed.

Susan: At the beginning of *Waiting for Saskatchewan* you write that the haibun is "short prose written from a haiku sensibility and, in this case, concluded by an informal haiku line" ("A Prefatory Note" *Waiting for Saskatchewan* n.p.). Can you talk a bit more about how the haibun and the haiku are related?

Fred: Formally, a haibun is supposed to end with a haiku. So if you're writing this short piece of prose and you know that you've got to end it with a little haiku, that's going to be in your consciousness as you're working through the piece; you're looking for the haiku sensibility—of fragility, seasonality, deep reflection, meditation—in the language. And you'd be paying attention to where these might be coming from. For example, one of the haibun ("Father/Mother Haibun #7") illustrates this: "Roads nearly empty, only a few pickups with firewood" (81). Even hearing that now I feel such a depth of sentiment—it's an image that comes from the fall, the autumn, when you're gathering firewood out in the Kootenays: not that many vehicles on the road, late Sunday afternoon, people going home for dinner, coming back from the bush late with your load of birch that you've scummed off of some logging site. My father died in September and I came out from Buffalo for his funeral, but just for the weekend—I had to go back to my studies. I remember not really making any contact with the place, with Nelson. I remember waking up on the morning of his funeral, and seeing fresh snow on Elephant Mountain, right across the lake from the city, and that's kind of a signal: here comes fall, here comes the winter. Starting in September you'd get snow on the mountain peaks. And it would come lower and lower and lower. And by November you'd have snow in Nelson:

> I was back in Buffalo when you died and when I came out
> for your funeral at the end of September there was snow
> on Elephant Mountain as far down as Pulpit Rock from
> Ernie's house the lake quiet my mother alone suddenly,
> months unused, unusual, I knew you best in the winter
> when there was curling and hockey or in the summer when
> we fished, dark mornings on the way to work or wet leaves
> in the gutter, driving at this time of year from Cranbrook
> to Nelson for the Lion's dance, car heater toasty warm
> upholstery, outside the air wet and cool mist hackles in
> the mountains your life simply closing down in the quiet
> month on the Hume Hotel ballroom floor wobble of the
> planet's sun seasons shortened golden flower's corny harvest
> elixir completed.

> **Road's nearly empty, only a few pickups with firewood.**
> ("Father/Mother Haibun #7" 81)

What I'm picking up on for the haiku at the end of that line is the sense of seasonality, and the melancholy of the seasons comes in for me really heavily in the fall.

Susan: Even before your dad died?

Fred: I can't remember. I suppose it did. It's something about growing up in Nelson. Of course this is a reflective process, since I was writing about his death fifteen years after, picking up on certain things, looking for a little nugget of haiku sensibility in the prose. If you read Japanese haibun, you see this haiku train coming down this piece of prose, you can feel it. You're trying to get the feeling of the haiku in the prose. You write the prose so that the haiku will appear out of the prose. But I found the project of inserting my mother as a content doesn't work in "This Dendrite Map." The address to my mother is rather sentimental, historical. It doesn't become problematized the way voicing my father becomes problematized. Because voicing the "you" of my father is also the reflective "you" of the poet's lyric "I" talking back to all the others.

Susan: What do you mean by reflective?

Fred: It reflects back, like a mirror, it's reflective. As well as deliberately referring to yourself. I discovered this—in a sense I discovered prose for myself—in writing *Grasp the Sparrow's Tail*, the utaniki where I'm writing a prose journal, a poetic journal made up of a lot of prose.* Some of the prose is more poetic than the so-called poem. But in *Grasp the Sparrow's Tail* I used the "you" as an address, an interpellation, hey you, hey you father. Speaking directly to another person:

> You never did the "horse" like I do now but walked
> straight down the aisle of the Diamond Grill
> and kicked the kitchen door with such a slap
> all the way up to the soda fountain
> I know it's you.
> (*Waiting* 31)

So it's epistolary in that sense. But then I realized in the next piece—there are two pieces there, in *Grasp the Sparrow's Tail*—where the "you" first appears. The direct I/you. Poet's voice talking to you the father. The next piece, in the Datong caves, the "you" gets mixed up (*Waiting* 49–51). It does a time-lapse thing, and you don't know whether the "you" is reflective or interpellative.

Susan: "Father/Mother Haibun #9" is really interesting because it's the only one that exceeds its own form.

Fred: Yeah. That's kind of a collage haibun. It's fragments.

Susan: Unlike the others, it's two pages long, and it's the only one that ends, not with one long line, but with three centered lines:

---

* Privately published in a small edition in Kyoto in 1982 and reprinted in *Waiting for Saskatchewan* 29–56.

Hannah Elizabeth
fell asleep in Jesus Arms
1918–1936
(*Waiting* 84)

After I read those lines I wondered if the haikus at the end of all the haibuns were epitaphs of some kind. And it's so different from all the others; it has dialogue but it's hard to tell who is speaking:

> "Why do you think of your father so much?"
> "He's dead. Every once in a while I think I see him, or someone I see reminds me of him, or I'm writing this book and he's in it."
> "That's not the truth. There's more to it than that."
> "What we'll try for is a paradigm in this."
> (*Waiting* 83)

At first I thought it was the mother speaking: "Why do you think of your father so much." I thought the mother was asking the questions, was the "Interrogator." Is that one layer?

Fred: I really don't know who's speaking. I mean, it is called "Father/ Mother Haibun."

Susan: Yes, and that is why I was looking for the mother. When I found this passage I remember thinking, there she is.

Fred: Compositionally, that is why it's a failed poem. It tries to insert the mother as a content, and the mother's voice, but that voice gets juxtaposed as the "you" does in the other focalization of relationship so it becomes more of a free floater in the poem. At least in that section.

Susan: At the end there's a reference to the "epitaph to my Aunt Hannah's grave in Swift Current. / It's like a song. Whenever I think of it I can hear my / Granny Wah singing, front row, in the Salvation Army hall" (*Waiting* 84). So you've returned not to your mother or her mother, but to your father's mother, to your father's side of the family.

Fred: Hannah Elizabeth was my father's sister. She died at 18 of an illness. It was after my father came back from China; he was 22– 23. So she's a younger sister to him, maybe 15–16. He came back and she took a shine to him. She helped him with his English. He often talked of Hannah as an important person to him. When I was back in Swift Current for a family reunion one year I went to the cemetery where my grandfather and grandmother were buried and found Hannah's grave next to them. And that's what it says on the gravestone. That would be the kind of thing my Granny Wah would say, metaphorical Salvation Army literalism of Christianity.

Susan: So we've veered away from the mother again. Why do you think that is?

Fred: I guess part of it's because my mother's alive so there's different imagery.

Susan: Do you think it has anything to do with the fact that she is white?

Fred: Well, my Granny was white.

Susan: But it's still on your father's side.

Fred: I don't think that kind of racialization occurred within the family because we had such a mix, such a variety of people. My father's brothers and sisters—some married Chinese, some married Scots, Irish.

Susan: Through your recent attempt to understand your identification with your father you've taken on race and racism. But your father was part white too. Do you have any interest in taking on your whiteness?

Fred: I guess what it's brought me to is not so much "taking on my whiteness" as a lever. By taking on the Chinese, the father thing, I've been trying to see what it is I'm taking on racially. In the last few years I've been more interested in the hyphen, the in-between, in figuring out how that works, what goes on at that site. Just as I know that I can't claim "the Chinese" as some pure envelope for my consciousness, I couldn't claim "white" either. But also because whiteness has always been the dominant, it has never been something that I really wanted to push out there because I was always suspicious of being white. A better question might be, "Am I suspicious of the mother?"

Susan: Are you?

Fred: Her family came from Sweden. They came as part of the working-class. As I was growing up everything was about class. It wasn't race or ethnicity at all, it was just class.

Susan: And your parents would have been working-class, both of them?

Fred: Very much so. The majority of Canadians were working-class. But the culture we were being fed in school wasn't working-class culture. It was European culture that excluded my father. So in a sense I've always felt my mother's history is taken care of, accounted for. But when I started writing about my father in the late 1970s there had been very little writing in Canada about the Chinese experience at all. No Chinese writers published in Canada. There had been one novel, written in Chinese, in Alberta, about the Chinese experience in Canada and I don't even know if it was translated. I knew of one or two poets in Vancouver but they'd never been published. If you think back on Asian history in Canada, the Japanese Canadians were much more articulate and much more forthcoming, much more productive, if you like, in terms of producing artifacts about their culture. Although they too were silenced during the internment. But the Chinese were silenced pretty totally from 1923 on—politically, socially, and finally, culturally. They just were not wanted. Of course any Chinese kid would not want to produce anything cultural and I didn't produce poetry because I was Chinese. But at a certain point it becomes possible to write poetry because you are Chinese. Very recently I read, in *Rice Paper* magazine, confessionals from young writers now thanking the Asian Canadian literary community for giving them the opportunity to tell their stories. There's now a whole industry around hyphenated Asian culture in North America, all around the world, the diasporic machine.

Susan: I'm probably pushing you to talk about your relation to your white mother because I'm a white feminist. Have you ever thought about how your experience might have been different if your mother had been Chinese and your father had been white?

Fred: I have met many people in that situation. But of course they have white names and no trace, no visible trace, of race. I'm curious, though, how does a feminist read *Diamond Grill*?

Susan: I read it as an interrogation of the ambiguous relation one has to privilege if, say, one's race is privileged and one's gender isn't, or vice versa. And as a moving articulation of a desire that is difficult to acknowledge: that one's privilege in one category excludes one's connection to the community to which one also belongs, but is separated from, by that very privilege. It gave me a way to think about such places in my own life. I was interested in your relationship to your white mother because for a white feminist interested in issues of race there's that moment when you realize that yes you are white, but you're still a woman. You're afforded privileges in the context of race but not of gender. That's why I wonder if you're conscious of inheriting both a history of racism from your father as well as a legacy of patriarchal privilege, since as the first son you were also born into a place of at least some power and certainly with considerable expectations that you take on the responsibilities associated with your place in the family.

Fred: This fall [2001] Roy Miki was teaching *Diamond Grill* at Simon Fraser. And since I was in Vancouver he asked me to come. It's a small upper-level, 400 level English class and really interesting because there were about eighteen students in the class and seventeen were women; sixteen Asian; seventeen Asian-Canadian; and one of them Korean.

Susan: What did they make of it?

Fred: Well, most of them loved it, they really enjoyed it and they had lots to talk about because most of the Chinese kids had heard similar stories from their parents. The food, the recipes. But then, the Korean student really shocked me. She said, in class, "Why did I treat the women so poorly?" That took me aback and I said, "Excuse me, I consciously tried not to treat them poorly. I tried consciously to represent the women in this story as very powerful, as having a lot to do with how the family's story moves along."

Susan: Did she draw your attention to anything in particular?

Fred: She was talking about the oppression of women by patriarchy. But I addressed that issue too when I talked about what a bastard my grandfather was and how these men treated women. She didn't read it that way. She was just seeing these characters as being pummelled down by the patriarchal.... I said, yes that's true but it's not that I'm trying to represent that. And I cited one or two pieces about my mother and my mother's family and how complicated that was racially, the fact that she was kicked out of the house. Her family didn't want anything to do with

her for marrying a Chinaman. And then she came up at the end
of the class and said, "You'll have to excuse me, I'm very much
a feminist."

Susan: It's a complicated and very layered text too so your readers
are never hit over the head with the issues you're taking on.

Fred: This subject, the father, the Chinese thing, is very ambiguous
for me. It involves working at identity. Of course I have no sure
ground from which to speak because I'm not Chinese. I didn't
grow up Chinese. I'm not Swedish...so my decision to forward
those anecdotes, to forward that story, to foreground the cafe
means foregrounding a place that is frequently ambivalent
for me. Because it involves memory and I'm bringing these
memories up into a late 80s, early 90s awareness of race and
culture. It's not that I have something I'm trying to say.

Susan: In the epigraph to *Diamond Grill* you write, "when you're
not pure you just make it up."

Fred: I was just thinking of that last night because I was trying to
write a preface for *Faking It*. The term "faking it" comes from
improvisation. In music, particularly in trumpet playing, you
fake it. In fact, one of the big books of music for jazz musicians
is *The Fake Book*. You see, there's the Real Book and then there's
the Fake Book. I'm beginning the book with a little essay called
"Faking It" that explains that when you're faking it you're doing
it out of necessity, you're not doing it just to have fun. There's
a pressure, a force there. It's the same as when you're playing
jazz. I've been reading a paper Miriam Nichols gave at ACCUTE
on bp and Daphne that takes to task the criticism that Nichol
and Marlatt have been receiving from the younger generation
of poets.[*] That paper sort of explained my own poetics to me.
It talks about the poetics of process as opposed to the poetics of
knowledge. Miriam points out that many of bp and Daphne's
detractors have been seeing their poetry from the point of view
of a poetry of knowing, whereas they have been involved in
a phenomenological poetry as opposed to an epistemological
one. A phenomenological approach is an approach to acquiring
knowledge but it insists on certain principles of experience.
It's a knowing by experience. I've always been interested in

[*] Later published as "Subjects of Experience."

discovering what I know through language. And in finding out what I don't know. To know what you don't know—I've always been fascinated by that. So "faking it" has been a really useful model for me.

Susan: You foreground the concept in the title of your new book of critical essays, called *Faking It*.

Fred: Yes but I call it a critical scrapbook.

Susan: Does that notion of the "scrapbook" give you another way of articulating hybrid subjectivity?

Fred: In some of my more recent essays like "Speak My Language: Racing the Lyric Poetic" it's about the lyric and how the lyric provides a complication for writers of colour, writers of race. I ask why does Evelyn Lau write these fairly mainstream, standard lyrics and others not? What are those choices? And I got quite interested in trying to figure that one out. I had a lot of fun with the lyric.

Susan: But if the "I" in a poem, the lyric subject, has been constructed as not racialized, can we assume there is such a thing as a racialized subject, in the history of poetry, even in the twentieth century?

Fred: That's an interesting question. But I think that there is, there implicitly has to be, a racialized subject that is a lyric "I." A writer like Annharte looks for that "I" to speak from. She and Jam Ismail have found a kind of energetic, vibrant position between the assumed lyric "I," the unquestioned lyric "I," and the more provocative, roughed lyric "I." But when I read someone like Rita Wong, I see someone who's consciously trying to find ways to move between those possibilities. Because narrative that so implicates that singular, solid "I" is hard to avoid. Particularly when you're trying to retell or remake the story. So it's a more useable "I."

Susan: What about the theory that none of us really uses the "I"; we might think we're using it but it's always using us.

Fred: As a writer I feel conscious of that.

Susan: But especially in terms of race no matter what you do, even if you try to racialize it, because of its history, it's going to erase you. It's not going to let you speak.

Fred: It's the only way to speak. There's no way around it. How else would one speak? The poetics of equivocation involves moving among these options. One always tries to find new corners of it. But it's not a totally new location. Formally, you're caught in the enunciation of it. Take Jeff Derksen for example, someone who wants to write totally outside of it yet writes a poem. Well you can't. So you write a poem, and all poems have the sense of someone, something speaking.

Susan: But with his work you can't settle the "I" down.

Fred: No, but it still carries and is still troubling the "I" that isn't present. But it's the "I" that isn't present that's present, if you see what I mean.

Susan: But don't you think your *Music at the Heart of Thinking* has the least sense of a speaking voice?

Fred: Probably.

Susan: How does that work in the writing process?

Fred: It's looking for other aspects, other formalisms. Jeff does this too in other ways, in which you just ignore the "I." You say to yourself, I'm not going to bother with that. I'm going to look at other aspects of this language being on the page doing something, saying something.

Susan: Do you think you can still take on race in that process?

Fred: Yes, racialization is language. It's a matter of engaging with diction, rewritings, and redefinitions.

Susan: Maybe this is a good time to look at the "Race, to Go" poem. Can you read it?

Fred: Sure.

What's yr race
        and she said
what's yr hurry
how 'bout it cock
                asian man
I'm just going for curry.

You ever been to ethni-city?
How 'bout multi-culti?

    You ever lay out skin
    for the white gaze?

What are you, banana
or egg? Coconut
maybe?

Something wrong Charlie
Chim-chong-say-wong-lung-chung?
You got a slant to yr marginal eyes?

You want a little rice with that garlic?
Is this too hot for you?

   Or slimy or bitter or smelly or tangy or raw or sour
— a little too dirty

   on the edge ~~hiding underneath~~ crawling up yr leg stuck
between the fingernails?

Is that a black hair in yr soup?

Well how you wanna handle this?
You wanna maintain a bit of differ-énce?
Keep our mother's other?
Use the father for the fodder?

What side of John A. MacDonald's tracks you on anyway?

How fast you think this train is going
                           to go?

Susan: I've never seen you use puns so intensely, that ironic—even
hybridised—difference between what you hear—"Caucasian"
man—and what you see on the page—"cock / asian" man. The
signifer suspends us between being white and being Asian, it
signifies a "cock"-"asian"—a white/asian man.
Fred: I'm just trying to play here. It's a performative poem.
Susan: What do you mean by that?
Fred: It's kind of jazzy and...
Susan: And really angry!

Fred: Yes, but it's jivey, this is a jivey poem. Even the way I spell it. Do you "wanna" maintain a bit of difference. Not do you "want to."

Susan: But you're bringing in the theoretical vocabulary with this really ordinary speech.

Fred: Yeah, but it's kind of colloquial, "you ever lay out skin for the white gaze."

Susan: What kind of a "she" is this—the "she" who says all this? The "she" who says, "what's your hurry"?

Fred: It's just picking up on a kind of male-female thing, playing around. Both "cock" sexually and the rooster, "cocky." It's not that she's saying this whole thing.

Susan: Is she white? I assumed she wasn't. The "he" is saying, "what's yr race"—and that could be taken seriously. Is he asking, "What race are you?"

Fred: I think it's mixed. Just mixed. Yeah, I guess she is raced there. But she could simply be someone who's aware.

Susan: But what about the line "keep *our* mother's other" (emphasis mine)? There seems to be a kind of collusion between them there.

Fred: No—this is Canada. The motherland. This is John A. MacDonald. The father.

Susan: But I thought it was about claiming the mother against the father, like the mother tongue against the dominant tongue.

Fred: I don't think so. It's about handling the mix, the difference, the apprehension of something hiding underneath.

Susan: Whose apprehension?

Fred: The white apprehension.

Susan: In both senses—being fearful of and understanding?

Fred: Yeah, the kind of apprehension of difference as being, in this case Asian, playing around with the restaurant, the food.

Susan: Class too? The other side of John A. Macdonald's tracks?

Fred: Yes.

Susan: How do you see your relationship to nationalism then?

Fred: I have this really ambivalent relation to nationalism. In one sense, I've always been violently anti-nationalist. Because of its preconception of who I was, who I am in it. It goes back to that question, what are you, Chinese or Canadian. Well, I'm Canadian. But you can't be. You're Chinese. This confusion about nationalism. Also the sense that this nation was made out of the apple of John A. MacDonald's eye. He just said, I want a nation, sea to shining sea, put these tracks across it and that's what's going to hold it together. So I really resist, don't like, that sense of place. I've always been more local, and oppositional to national things. The machinations of it, the mechanics, the dynamics of nationalism force me to take it on. The fact that as a writer I have to go to Ottawa to argue about public lending rights, copyright and so forth, that it's controlled there. It really is.

Susan: That you can't just ignore it. It's functioning.

Fred: As Roy Miki says, the "there" is "here." I'm not anti-nationalist to the extent that I'm going to deny that there is a there.

Susan: You're not just working outside of that institution.

Fred: No, not totally. But I'm always ready to trouble it, trouble the assumption that it's a given for one thing.

Susan: Is the fact that you can ask these questions a product of Canadian nationalism? After all, questions of race weren't being asked in the 1950s, and then in the 1960s people were suddenly talking about bilingualism and multiculturalism and it's no accident that at that moment Canadian policy was changing on those subjects.

Fred: Well this morning on e-mail Andrea Strudensky asked me a provocative question. She said that she's doing something on Dennis Lee; she's reading *Body Music* where Lee claims that "we" poets, meaning "we Canadian poets," between 1955 and 1965 had this infatuation with and inferiority complex in relation to American poets. That we worshipped them from afar. And Andrea wrote to me and said, this doesn't make sense. She said she knew I was involved with this group on the west coast, the TISH thing and all that. She said that it seemed what I was doing contradicts what Lee was doing. So I wrote back to her and said that Lee's using himself to represent a "we"—Atwood, himself, Northrop Frye, House of Anansi—that assumes that when they speak from their position they're speaking for all Canadian poets. I never assumed that. On the west coast I was more interested in American poets, not because I was infatuated with them or saw them from afar; in fact we brought them into Vancouver, we talked to them, I went down to the States to study, it was very concrete. Anyway, we talked about that "we"—that Canadian "we"—and I've never had that sense

of the "we" that Dennis Lee assumes, yet I realize it's there.
The "we" is multiple. Not to make Dennis take total responsibility. There's that centrist "we" that assumes representation.
And there's another "we." A more local "we" that questions the
larger one. And in fact resists it with something more personal
and geographically more local. But that's an old contention.
James Reaney and the regionalists in London did that too. To get
them away from Toronto.

Susan: Do you think that the official policy of multiculturalism is
a delayed response on the part of the government to something
that's happening already at the local level?

Fred: Not a delayed response, a delaying response. It's a way to
delay the there being here, let's keep it out there. Official multiculturalism is one way of containing it.

Susan: So you don't think there's any sense in which an official
government policy would be enabling for writers of colour?

Fred: Oh it's very enabling for us to a degree, in that it throws
money, funds, publishing, recognition; but then those voices
become controlled by a cultural machine that is very much
manipulated by a sense of nationalism.

Susan: That can happen, but does it always happen? With you? And
Roy Miki?

Fred: Oh it does happen. I'm writing a paper with Smaro
Kamboureli on the "Race Poetry, eh?" issue of *Prairie Fire* (21.4)
funded by the Department of Canadian Heritage for the United
Nations' anti-racism day.* Hedy Fry** said that they wanted
something to take to Durban. What the Department of Canadian
Heritage—which was more interested in global trade, or global
representation of Canadian culture—wanted to foreground was
race poetry. They paid for 1,800 copies of *Prairie Fire*. Meanwhile
in Canada, they shrink-wrap this volume and send it out with
their general issue. In Canada what you see is the "race" issue
and the "general" issues side by side, shrink-wrapped. Fred Wah,
Rita Wong, etc. are shrink-wrapped along with the general issue.
Yet the attempt was made to package "Race Poetry" outside of
Canada. Unfortunately, it was a little too hot. It was a solidly

---

* International Day for the Elimination of Racial Discrimination on March 21, 2001.
** Then Secretary of State for Multiculturalism and the Status of Women.

political issue. Hedy Fry in her one page introduction quotes a poem by Thuong Vuong-Riddick: "It is this human warmth / of the country / I belong to" (2)—and you think ugh, that's kind of sucky. And, come on Ash,* why did you choose that. But then you find out that the poem is not even in the volume. But since she cites it, it makes you think it must be. Anyway, there's this whole problem of being articulated through a Canadian nationalism. On the other hand, there's funding for *Prairie Fire* so that an Ashok Mathur can get this issue going; there's greater awareness of race writing in Canada. I was just reading an essay by Charles Foran in Air Canada's magazine arguing that through Michael Ondaatje, Neil Bissoondath, "Global lit," Canada has come of age in world literature. When you look at what's read out there—Atwood, Ondaatje, Rohinton Mistry, Visanjy, Anita Badami—these are stories, narratives, that occur in some other place, with a little Canadian seasoning. So they give the sense that race happens someplace else. And yes, these are good Canadian writers because they can talk about their homeland elsewhere.

Susan: How do you see the relationship between poetry and social change?

Fred: Since the 1970s I've believed that poetry is only interesting if it has to do with change. I didn't always think of social change, at first I was thinking of individual change of consciousness or change of awareness. Some of that goes back to before the 1970s and working with [Charles] Olson and his notion of what's right, right value…

Susan: …ethics?

Fred: Ethics. An ethics and that goes back to writing *Earth* in the late 1960s and early 1970s:

> Eth means why any one returns
> every one all over the place they are in
> entwined into the confluence of the two rivers
> into the edges of a genetic inscription
> and our homes and loves now night
> spreads out up the valleys

* The issue was edited by Ashok Mathur.

into the many-forgotten messages and arrangements
carried there the character sticks
hunger

I was writing out of the sense of eth as ethos as home. Earth is home.

Susan: But home is such a domesticated concept, so constructed.

Fred: Remember Gary Snyder's book *Earth House Hold*—yeah it was domestic, and that was the whole thing, looking after the earth. But I'm playing with it here from an Olson angle. Eth as home but related to home as the place that one can imagine. In the same sense that Olson talks about New England; the founding fathers of New England saw Boston as a shining beacon on the hill that would give light and direction to everyone around, that sense of Image Nation, imagination, the kind of world one would want to live in, the kind of earth. It's about ethics because there are right ways and wrong ways. And you have to know how to be right.

Susan: Do you see it as that absolute?

Fred: No, but I see it as activated at the level of the domestic.

Susan: I'm not sure what you mean.

Fred: The domestic has to do with looking after.

Susan: So being on the earth is a kind of primary domesticity?

Fred: Yes. You have to look after where you are. And ethics, the implications through Olson are that...

Susan: Writing poetry is a way of looking after where you are?

Fred: Yes. You have an ethical responsibility to language, change and social change. I say to my students, a little too rambunctiously perhaps, I don't know why you'd want to write a poem if it wasn't meant to change the world you live in. And they all think, well that's kind of high falutin' and they make these quips, and say things like, "Well, here's my little poem. I don't mean to change the world with it or anything." In a sense they don't get it. They think I'm trying to make poetry elitist. But it's not—it's the kind of ethics I'm talking about and why I found Olson so useful in the sense that belief and ethics were being brought into poetry. Before that, I thought poetry was just this neat thing, this beautiful little thing in our culture. But no. It was the first indication I had that poetry might be for the imagination, and the imagination might be used to bring about worlds.

Susan: Have you seen shifts in your thinking over the past 30 or 40 years?

Fred: I've seen shifts more recently in the last 15 or 20 years. It's become possible to articulate some of those "right" values as having to do with identity, as having to do with who I am and with wanting to take position. In the early 1960s it wasn't necessary for me to take a position on, let's say, race. Let's just say I could pass. But even those who couldn't pass wouldn't take a position. Sonny [Wayson] Choy was at UBC the same time we were and he was one of the only Chinese students in the arts at UBC in 1960 and he wasn't taking a position. Certain notions of social change just weren't possible. Now a writer like Dionne Brand comes to her writing almost fully set-up...

Susan: ...politically conscious, you mean?

Fred: Yes, she writes to effect social change.

Susan: Yes, because she was a political activist right from the beginning.

Fred: I wasn't. I came to that later. But I believe that writing is only interesting if it offers possibilities for shifts in consciousness, and hopefully shifts in the way we experience the world.

Susan: Has your participation in various communities been linked to your own changes in consciousness?

Fred: Well the TISH poets' notions of class brought us to a sense of rebellion, subversion. We were this group of young poets at UBC who saw that a more elite group of writers were swarming around up top. So that was a social thing, although not really informed about itself as social. We were influenced by the 1960s notion of heterogeneity. We [his wife Pauline Butling and himself] went back to the West Kootenays in the late 1960s and believed in the notion of community as the prime social value. Our friends were forming communes and living with one another. Our closest alliance to any writing community was in Vancouver, with the York Street Commune (Stan Persky, Brian de Beck, Gladys Hindmarch, and Lanny Beckman). They formed New Star Press. A whole culture in Vancouver developed around the York Street Commune.

Susan: Wherever you live you find or create a writing community. Obviously you see working in community as productive.

Fred: Yes, I've always worked in community. I've always felt that's where writing belongs, in getting together with people to produce work.

Susan: So the community matters because of the connections it makes at that really local level, because it brings people together?

Fred: Not just at that local level though. Particularly now, the new technologies make a wider dialogue possible. While I was in Thailand on sabbatical last winter (2001) I wrote a long piece centred around a paper that Hank Laser had written on Ron Silliman. He sent it to me just before I went to Thailand and I took it along because it was xeroxed. I didn't want to take books. It was fascinating. So part of what I wrote were these letters to Hank that talk a little bit about poetry and some of his ideas and [Ron] Silliman's ideas, etc. Larger communities of like-minded people are out there as you know, particularly in the academic world. And that is becoming true for the literary world too. More conferences are drawing writers together. So there's this incredible network all over the world. I was reading something by James Sherry, the New York Language poet, that was given to me by Zhang Ziquing in Nanjing, China in 1996. I knew James Sherry before. But I hadn't had time to read it until now. And I thought it was really good so I wanted to write to James and ask him if I could use it for one of my classes. So I thought, I'll have to phone Louis [Cabri] and get James' e-mail address because of course I could be in touch with him by e-mail. So yes, community has been really, really important. Beginning with the notion of a group of people in the room producing a magazine to people sharing books and sharing ideas. Even working collaboratively. Like the collaboration I did with Bev Tosh. It gave me the opportunity to work with an artist, a visual artist who was doing something totally different from what I was doing and yet I could dovetail into it. She asked me to apply text to her paintings. I really enjoyed doing that and using some of the ideas and language and poetry around identity and race and change. If you look at the language in that series of poems there's an awful lot of playful, subtle stuff about identity. I'm also involved in another collaboration with Haruko Okano, a

Vancouver artist. We did a performance last fall in Banff and we did a performance this August in Vancouver on hybridity called "High(bridi)Tea" so it was called "High Tea."

Susan: When you say performance, what do you mean?

Fred: It's an event that involves a dinner table of 26 place settings. I wrote a piece called an "alphabet of contamination" which is a series of 26 cards with little jerky, quickie, trippy, word things on contamination, hybridity. And that has to do with an art form that involves fungus, mould, contamination. In Vancouver we turned this 26-place setting into a restaurant where she was a waitress and I was a waiter, and we would serve the people sitting at the table this language. And we would have another dialogue going on between ourselves talking about the cafe and about what we were serving. That was all improvised. A door has become an important aspect of the performance. On one side of the door is the kitchen; on the other side is the cafe where the customers are. And the languages in those two areas are different. She's discovered a pidgin Japanese-Canadian language that came out of the internment camps, so she's playing with that. In the first one, I published a little envelope of green cards. We did a little chapbook of these cards that we gave away to the audience at the first performance. For the last performance, I did a menu of hybridity that contained a lot of the same language as the cards. And Haruko did a beautiful chapbook, a limited edition of fifty. Each of us had a waitress' bill pad that we would fake writing on; we'd give people bills with her language on it. At the end of the performance her bill pad, which was I think fifty-two pages long, was nailed on the wall and people could go up and put together chapbooks. We gave them covers and had a big stapler ready. It was a beautiful production. Next week, I'm going to do a little collaboration with Peter Bartl, this printer and graphic designer from Edmonton who did *Limestone Lakes Utaniki* produced by Red Deer College Press. Peter has a place near our place at Kootenay Lake. He's set up a print studio with a letterpress and six-inch wooden letters. Then I'm doing something with a photographer, Marian Penner Bancroft in Vancouver. The show is already up but they want text for it, for a catalogue, and they'd like a poetic text. So if we get the money I'll go do that. Working with visual artists is all open, new ground and I love it.

Works Cited

Annharte [Marie Annharte Baker]. Author's Note. Goldie and
    Moses 368.
———. "Backburner." *West Coast Line* 20, 30.2 (1996): 150.
———. *Being on the Moon*. Winlaw, B.C.: Polestar Press, 1990.
———. "Borrowing Enemy Language: A First Nation's Woman's
    Use of English." *West Coast Line* 10, 27/2 (1993): 59–66.
———. *Coyote Columbus Cafe*. Winnipeg: Moonprint, 1994.
———. "Coyote Columbus Cafe." *Coyote Columbus Cafe* 11–17.
    Rpt. Armstrong and Grauer 71–76.
———. *Exercises in Lip Pointing*. Vancouver: New Star, 2003.
———. "Marie Annharte Baker." Armstrong & Grauer 63.
———. "Medicine Lines: The Doctoring of Story and Self."
    Canadian Women's Studies / les cahiers de la femme 14.2
    (Spring 1994): 114–18.
Armah, Ayi Kwei. *The Beautyful [sic] Ones Are Not Yet Born*.
    Boston: Houghton Mifflin, 1968.
Armstrong, Jeannette C. and Lally Grauer, eds. *Native Poetry in
    Canada: A Contemporary Anthology*. Peterborough, Ontario:
    Broadview Press, 2001.
Atwood, Margaret, ed. *The New Oxford Book of Canadian Verse
    in English*. Toronto; New York: Oxford University Press, 1982.
Bailey, Norma. *Cowboys and Indians: The Killing of J.J. Harper*
    (videorecording). Producers: Eric Jordan and Jeremy Torrie
    (Ojibway). The Film Works Ltd. and High Definition Pictures
    in association with APTN and CBC, 2003.

Baker, Marie Annharte. *See* Annharte.

Banting, Pamela. *Body, Inc. A Theory of Translation Poetics.*
Winnipeg: Turnstone, 1995.

Barbour, Douglas. *Daphne Marlatt and Her Works.* Toronto: ECW
Press, n.d.

———, ed. *Beyond* TISH*: New Writing, Interviews, Critical Essays.*
Spec. Issue of *West Coast Line* 25.1 (Spring 1991). Co-published
Edmonton: NeWest, 1991.

Barnholden, Michael and Andrew Klobucar, eds. *Writing Class:
The Kootenay School of Writing Anthology.* Vancouver: New
Star, 1999.

Barthes, Roland. *Writing Degree Zero.* Trans. Annette Lavers,
Colin Smith, Susan Sontag. New York: Hill and Wang, 1953.

Beddoes, Julie. "Mastering the Mother Tongue: Reading Frank
Davey Reading Daphne Marlatt's *How Hug a Stone.*" *Canadian
Literature* 155 (Winter 1997): 75–87.

Bennett, Donna and Russell Brown, eds. *A New Anthology of
Canadian Literature in English.* Don Mills: Oxford UP, 2002.

Benson, Eugene and L.W. Conolly, eds. *Routledge Encyclopedia of
Post-Colonial Literatures in English.* London: Routledge, 1994.

Bertacco, Simona. *Out of Place: The Writings of Robert Kroetsch.*
Bern, Switzerland: Peter Lang, 2002.

Besner, Neil, Deborah Schnitzer, and Alden Turner, eds.
Uncommon Wealth: An Anthology of Poetry in English.
Toronto: Oxford UP, 1997.

Black, Ayanna, ed. *Fiery Spirits: Canadian Writers of African
Descent.* n.p.: HarperPerennial, 1995.

Blaser, Robin. "The Practice of Outside." In Blaser, ed. 271–329.

Blaser, Robin, ed. *The Collected Books of Jack Spicer.* Los Angeles:
Black Sparrow, 1975.

Bowering, George. *Kerrisdale Elegies.* Toronto: Coach House, 1984.

Brathwaite, J. Ashton / Odimumba Kwamdela. *Black British
Soldier.* Brooklyn, N.Y.: Kibo Books, 1986.

———. *Niggers…This Is Canada.* Toronto: 21st Century Books, 1971.

Brand, Dionne. "A Conceptual Analysis of how Gender Roles
are Racially Constructed." M.A. Thesis, Ontario Institute for
Studies in Education, University of Toronto, 1988.

———. *A Map to the Door of No Return: Notes to Belonging.*
Toronto: Doubleday Canada, 2001.

———. *At The Full & Change Of The Moon.* Toronto: Alfred A. Knopf Canada, 1999.

———. "Black Women in Toronto: Gender, Race and Class." *Fireweed: A Feminist Quarterly* 19 (Summer/Fall 1984): 26–43.

———. *Bread Out of Stone: recollections sex recognitions race dreaming politics.* Toronto: Coach House, 1994.

———. *Chronicles of the Hostile Sun.* Toronto: Williams-Wallace, 1984.

———. *Earth Magic.* Toronto: Kids Can Press, 1979.

———. *'Fore Day Morning: Poems.* Toronto: Khoisan Artists, 1978.

———. *In Another Place, Not Here.* Toronto: Alfred A. Knopf Canada, 1996.

———. "Interview with Dionne Brand: Owning the language." By Lynne Wankeki, Nikola Maria De Marin and Charmaine Perkins. *Kinesis,* October 1993: 20–21.

———. *Land to Light On.* Toronto: McClelland and Stewart, 1997.

———. *Listening for Something* [videorecording]: *Adrienne Rich and Dionne Brand in Conversation.* Studio D, National Film Board of Canada, 1996.

———. *Long time comin'* [videorecording]. New York: Women Make Movies, 1993.

———. *No Language Is Neutral.* Toronto: Coach House, 1990.

———. *Older, stronger, wiser* [videorecording]. Directed by Claire Prieto. Associate Director and Writer Dionne Brand. Montreal: National Film Board of Canada, 1989.

———. *Primitive Offensive.* Toronto: Williams-Wallace, 1982.

———. *Sans Souci and Other Stories.* Toronto: Williams-Wallace, 1988.

———. *Sisters in the Struggle* [videorecording]. Toronto: National Film Board of Canada, 1991.

———. *thirsty.* Toronto: McClelland and Stewart, 2002.

———.*Winter Epigrams & Epigrams to Ernesto Cardenal in Defense of Claudia.* Toronto: Williams-Wallace, 1983.

——— and Krisantha Sri Bhaggiyadatta. *Rivers Have Sources, Trees Have Roots: Speaking of Racism.* Toronto: Cross Cultural Communication Centre, 1986.

——— and Lois de Shield. *No Burden to Carry: Narratives of Black Working Women in Ontario 1920s to 1950s.* Toronto: Women's Press, 1991.

Bromige, David. "Intention & Poetry." In Perelman, ed. 25–49.

Brossard, Nicole. *The Aerial Letter*. Toronto: Women's Press, 1988.

———. "Articulation (sic) Deformation in Play." *Daydream Mechanics*. Trans. Larry Shouldice. Toronto: Coach House Quebec Translations, 1980. 61–71.

———. *Installations*. Trans. Erin Mouré and Robert Majzels. Winnipeg: Muses' Co., 2000.

———. *Museum of Bone and Water*. Trans. Robert Majzels and Erin Mouré. Toronto: Anansi, 2003.

———. *Under Tongue / Sous la langue*. Trans. Susanne de Lotbinière-Harwood. Charlottetown, P.E.I.: Gynergy and Montréal: L'Essentielle, 1987.

Budde, Robert. "After postcolonialism: migrant lines and the politics of form in Fred Wah, M. Nourbese Philip, and Roy Miki." In *Is Canada postcolonial? Unsettling Canadian literature*. Ed. Laura Moss. Waterloo: Wilfrid Laurier UP, 2003. 282–94.

Butling, Pauline. "'From Radical to Integral': Daphne Marlatt's 'Booking Passage'." Pauline Butling and Susan Rudy, *Writing in Our Time: Canada's Radical Poetries in English (1957–2003)*. Waterloo: Wilfrid Laurier UP, 2005.

——— and Susan Rudy. *Writing in Our Time: Canada's Radical Poetries in English (1957–2003)*. Waterloo: Wilfrid Laurier UP, 2005.

Cabri, Louis. " 'Diminishing the Lyric I': Notes on Fred Wah & the Social Lyric." *Open Letter* 12.3 (Fall 2004): 77–91.

Campbell, Maria. *Halfbreed*. Toronto: McClelland and Stewart, 1973.

Camper, Carol, ed. *Miscegenation Blues: Voices of Mixed Race Women*. Toronto: Sister Vision, 1994.

"A Canadian Issue." Spec. issue of *boundary 2, a journal of postmodern literature* 2 3.1 (Fall 1974): 1–249. [General Editor Robert Kroetsch. Poetry selected by Margaret Atwood and Warren Tallman. Criticism selected by Robert Kroetsch and Eli Mandel.]

Carr, Brenda. "Between Continuity and Difference: An Interview with Daphne Marlatt." In Barbour, ed. 99–107.

Carrière, Marie. *Writing in the feminine in French and English Canada: a question of ethics*. Toronto: U of Toronto P, 2002.

Cook, Meira. "Partisan body: performance and the female body in Dionne Brand's *No Language is Neutral*." *Open Letter* 9.2 (1995): 54–61.

Culleton, Beatrice. *April Raintree*. Winnipeg: Pemmican, 1984.

da Costa, Paulo. "Dionne Brand. An Interview with Paulo da Costa: The blood boils in Canada around the French/English conflict." *ciberkiosk—entrevista*.<www.ciberkiosk.pt/entrevista/brand.html>

Davey, Frank and bpNichol, eds. "Robert Kroetsch: Essays." *Open Letter* 5.4 (Spring 1983): 7–127.

Davey, Frank, Nicole Markotic and Susan Rudy, eds. "Fred Wah: Alley Alley Home Free." *Open Letter* 12.2 (Summer 2004): 1–131.

———. "Alley Alley Home Free Part 2." *Open Letter* 12.3 (Summer 2004): 1–135.

Davidson, Michael. "The Prose of Fact." In Perelman, ed. 166–83.

Davis, Kevin. *Pause Button*. Vancouver: Tsunami Editions, 1992.

Derksen, Jeff. "All Mod Contradictions" [manuscript title]. Retitled and published as Derksen, *Transnational Muscle Cars*.

———. *But Can I Make A Living From It*. Philadelphia/Vancouver: hole chapbooks, 2000.

———. *Down Time*. Vancouver: Talonbooks, 1990.

———. *Dwell*. Vancouver: Talonbooks, 1993.

———. "Fixed City & Mobile World: Urban Facts & Global Forces in Ken Lum's Art." *Ken Lum Works with Photography*. Eds. Kitty Scott and Martha Hanna. Ottawa: National Gallery of Canada, 2002. 31–43.

———. "Globalism and the Role of the Cultural: Nation, 'Multiculturalism,' and Articulated Locals." Ph.D. Diss. Department of English, University of Calgary, 2000.

———. "Making Race Opaque: Fred Wah's Poetics of Opposition and Differentiation." *West Coast Line* 29.3 (1995): 63–76.

———. *Memory Is the Only Thing Holding Me Back*. Nelson, B.C.: David Thompson UP, 1984.

———. *Selfish: Something Deep Inside Liberal Cultural Relativism Says "Yes I Can."* Vancouver: Pomflit, 1993.

———. "Sites Taken as Signs: Place, the Open Text, and Enigma in New Vancouver Writing." *Vancouver: Representing the Postmodern City*. Ed. Paul Delany. Vancouver: Arsenal Pulp, 1994. 144–61.

———. *Transnational Muscle Cars*. Vancouver: Talonbooks, 2003.

————. "Unrecognizable Texts: From Multicultural to Antisystemic Writing." *West Coast Line* 24, 31.3 (Winter 1997–98):
59–71. Rpt. in Wallace and Marks 145–160.

————. *Until*. Vancouver: Tsunami Editions, 1987; rpt. 1989.

————. Website: <http://www.lot.at/mynewidea_com>.

Derksen, Jeff, Sabine Bitter and Helmut Weber. "But is it Politics?"
website. <http://www.lot.at/politics>.

Derksen, Jeff and Ron Silliman. Phillytalks #3. 1998–01–02.
<slought.net/toc/archives/display2/php?key=PhillyTalks>

Derksen, Jeff, ed. "Disgust & Overdetermination: A Poetics Issue."
Open Letter 10.1 (Winter 1998).

Diehl-Jones, Charlene. *Fred Wah and His Works*. ECW Press:
Toronto, 1997.

di Michele, Mary, ed. *Anything is Possible: a selection of eleven
women poets*. Oakville: Mosaic Press, 1984.

Dickinson, Peter. "Orality in Literacy: Listening to Indigenous
Writing." *Canadian Journal of Native Studies* 14.2 (1994):
319–40.

Dickson, Lisa. "'Signals across boundaries': non-congruence and
Erin Mouré's 'Sheepish Beauty, Civilian Love'." *Canadian
Literature* 155 (1997): 16–38.

Dopp, Jamie. "'Field of potentialities': reading Erin Mouré." *Essays
on Canadian Writing* 67 (1999): 261–87.

Dybikowski, Ann, Victoria Freeman, Daphne Marlatt, Barbara
Pulling, Betsy Warland, ed. *In the feminine: Women & Words
/ les femmes et les mots: Conference Proceedings*. Edmonton:
Longspoon, 1985.

Edelman, Gerald. *The Remembered Present*. New York: Basic
Books, 1989.

Edwards, Brian. "Kroetsch, Robert Paul (1927–)." Benson and
Conolly. *http://gateway.proquest.com/*.

Fanon, Frantz. *The Wretched of the Earth*. New York: Grove, 1963.

Fitzgerald, Judith. "Thoughts on G-G poetry short list." *Globe &
Mail* (Toronto, Canada), November 15, 1997. p. D11.

Fry, Hedy. "Letter." In Mathur, "Race Poetry, Eh?" 2.

Geddes, Gary, ed. 15 *Canadian Poets x* 3. 4th edition. Don Mills:
Oxford UP, 2001.

————. *20th Century Poetry & Poetics*. 1st ed. Toronto: Oxford
UP, 1969.

————. *20th Century Poetry & Poetics*. 2nd ed. Toronto: Oxford
UP, 1973.

————. *20th Century Poetry & Poetics*. 3rd ed. Toronto: Oxford
UP, 1985.

————. *20th Century Poetry & Poetics*. 4th ed. Toronto: Oxford
UP, 1996.

Glancy, Diane and Mark Nowak, eds. *Visit Tepee Town: Native
Writings After the Detours*. Minneapolis: Coffee House, 1999.

Godard, Barbara. "Body I: Daphne Marlatt's Feminist Poetics."
Canadian Review of American Studies 15.4 (1985): 481–96.

————. "Other Fictions: Robert Kroetsch's Criticism." *Open Letter*
5.8–9 (Summer–Fall 1984): 5–21.

Goldie, Terrie and Daniel David Moses, eds. *An Anthology of
Canadian Native Literature in English*. Toronto: Oxford UP, 1992.

Gossett, Hattie. *Sister No Blues*. New York: Firebrand, 1988.

Grauer, Lally. "'The weasel pops in and out of old tunes': Marie
Annharte Baker as a Scavenger Poet." Unpublished paper, 2004.

Grenier, Robert. "On Speech" *This* 1 (Winter 1971): 82–83. Rpt. in
In the American Tree. Ed. Ron Silliman. Orono, ME: National
Poetry Foundation, 1986: 496–97.

Harjo, Joy. *What moon drove me to this?* New York: Reed Books,
1979.

Howe, Fanny. "Justice." In Perelman, ed. 184–89.

Huk, Romana, ed. *Assembling Alternatives: Reading Postmodern
Poetries Transnationally*. Middletown, Connecticut: Wesleyan
UP, 2003.

Hunter, Lynette. "After Modernism: Alternative Voices in the
Writings of Dionne Brand, Claire Harris, and Marlene Philip."
University of Toronto Quarterly 62.2 (Winter 1992): 256–81.

James, C.L.R. *The Black Jacobins: Toussaint L'Ouverture and the
San Domingo Revolution*. New York: Vintage Books, 1963.

————. *Minty Alley: a novel*. London: Secker and Warburg, 1936.

Jarraway, David. "Citizen Jane." Rev. of *thirsty* by Dionne Brand,
Spinoza in Her Youth by Norma Cole and *O Cidadán* by Erin
Mouré. *Arc* 49 (Winter 2002): 73–78.

Johanson, Reg. Rev. of *Exercises in Lip Pointing* by Annharte. *The
Rain: The Vancouver Review of Books* 1.1 (Sept/Oct 2003): n.p.

Kamboureli, Smaro. "Faking It: Fred Wah and the Postcolonial
Imaginary." *Études canadiennes/Canadian Studies: revue inter-*

disciplinaire des études canadiennes en France (Assn Française d'Études Canadiennes, Talence) 54 (2003): 115–32.

———, ed. *Making a Difference: Canadian Multicultural Literature.* Toronto: Oxford UP, 1996.

Knutson, Susan. "Deixis/Dreams." Rev. of *Installations* by Nicole Brossard, Trans. Erin Moure; *She would be the First Sentence of my Next Novel* by Nicole Brossard, Trans. Susanne de Lotbiniere-Harwood; *A Suit of Light* by Anne Hebert, Trans. Sheila Fischman. *Canadian Literature* 173 (Summer 2002): 124–27.

———. *Narrative in the Feminine: Daphne Marlatt and Nicole Brossard.* Waterloo: Wilfrid Laurier UP, 2000.

Kroetsch, Robert. *Advice to My Friends: A Continuing Poem.* Don Mills, Ontario: Stoddart, 1985.

———, ed. "A Canadian Issue." Spec. issue of *boundary* 2 3.1 (1974).

———. *Completed Field Notes: The Long Poems of Robert Kroetsch.* Toronto: McClelland and Stewart, 1989.

———. *Completed Field Notes: The Long Poems of Robert Kroetsch.* 2nd ed. with an introduction by Fred Wah. Edmonton: U of Alberta P, 2000.

———. "The Criminal Intensities of Love as Paradise." *Completed Field Notes* 81–93.

———. "Delphi: Commentary." *Open Letter* 5.8–9 (1984): 22–39. Rpt. in Kroetsch, *Completed Field Notes,* 2nd ed.: 213–36.

———. *Excerpts from the Real World.* Lantzville, B.C.: Oolichan Books, 1986.

———. *Field Notes 1–8 a continuing Poem: The Collected Poetry of Robert Kroetsch.* Don Mills, Ontario: General, 1981. Rpt. in Kroetsch, *Completed Field Notes,* 2nd ed.: 213–36.

———. "For Play and Entrance: The Contemporary Canadian Long Poem." Kroetsch, *The Lovely Treachery* 117–34.

———. *The Hornbooks of Rita K.* Edmonton: U of Alberta P, 2001.

———. "I Wanted to Write a Manifesto." Kroetsch, *A Likely Story* 41–64.

———. *The Ledger.* London, Ontario: Applegarth Follies, 1975. Rpt. in Kroetsch, *Completed Field Notes* 2nd ed.: 11–28.

———. *A Likely Story: the writing life.* Red Deer: Red Deer College P, 1995.

———. *The Lovely Treachery of Words: Essays Selected and New.* Toronto: Oxford UP, 1989.

———. *The Man from the Creeks.* Toronto: Random House, 1998.

———. "Poem for My Dead Sister." Kroetsch, *A Likely Story.* 157–70.

———. *The Puppeteer.* Toronto: Random House, 1992.

———. *Revisions of Letters Already Sent.* Calgary: DisOrientation Chapbooks, 1991.

———. *The Sad Phoenician.* Toronto: Coach House, 1979. Rpt. in Kroetsch, *Completed Field Notes* 2nd ed.: 51–65.

———. *Seed Catalogue.* 1977. Winnipeg: Turnstone, 1986.

———. *The Stone Hammer Poems: 1960–1975.* Nanaimo, B.C.: oolichan books, 1975.

———. *The Studhorse Man.* Toronto: Macmillan, 1969.

Laclau, Ernesto and Chantal Mouffe. *Hegemony and Socialist Strategy: Towards a Radical Democratic Politics.* Trans. Winston Moore and Paul Cammock. New York: Verso, 1985.

Lee, Dennis. *Body Music.* Toronto: Anansi, 1998.

Lew, Walter K., ed. *Premonitions: The Kaya Anthology of New Asian North American Poetry.* New York: Kaya Production, 1995.

Marlatt, Daphne. *Ana Historic.* Toronto: Coach House, 1988.

———. "At Birch Bay." *Net Work: Selected Writing* 133.

———. "Booking Passage." *Salvage* 111–19. Rpt. in Marlatt, *This Tremor Love Is.* Vancouver, Talonbooks: 69–72.

———. "Changing the Focus." *InVersions: Writings by Dykes, Queers & Lesbians.* Ed. Betsy Warland. Vancouver: Press Gang, 1991. 127–34.

———. *Frames of a Story.* Toronto: Ryerson, 1968.

———. "Given This Body: An Interview with Daphne Marlatt." By George Bowering. *Open Letter* 4.3 (Spring 1975): 32–88.

———. *Ghost Works.* Edmonton: NeWest, 1993.

———. *here & there.* Lantzville B.C.: Island Writing Series, 1981.

———. *How Hug a Stone.* Winnipeg: Turnstone, 1983.

———. "In the Month of Hungry Ghosts." *The Capilano Review* 16/17 (1979): 45–95.

———. *leaf leaf/s.* Los Angeles: Black Sparrow, 1969.

———. "Musing with Mothertongue (1982–1983)." Marlatt *Readings* 9–16.

———. *Net Work: Selected Writing.* Ed. Fred Wah. Vancouver: Talonbooks, 1980.

———. "Of the matter." Introduction. Marlatt, *What Matters.* n.p.

———. *Our Lives.* Carrborro, N.C.: Truck Press, 1975. Rpt. Lanzville B.C.: oolichan, 1980.

———. *Readings from the Labyrinth.* Edmonton: NeWest, 1998.

———. *Rings.* Vancouver: Georgia Straight Writing Supplement, 1971.

———. *Salvage.* Red Deer: Red Deer College P, 1991.

———. "Sea Haven." Rimanelli 332–72.

———, ed. *Steveston Recollected: a Japanese-Canadian History.* Victoria, B.C.: Aural History, Provincial Archives of British Columbia, 1975.

———. *Taken.* Concord, Ontario: House of Anansi, 1996.

———. *This Tremor Love Is.* Vancouver: Talonbooks, 2001.

———. *Touch to My Tongue.* Edmonton: Longspoon, 1984.

———. *Vancouver Poems.* Toronto: Coach House, 1972.

———. *What Matters: Writing 1968–1970.* Toronto: Coach House, 1980.

———. "When we change language…" Williamson 182–93.

———. *Zócalo.* Toronto: Coach House Press 1977.

Marlatt, Daphne and Betsy Warland. *Double Negative.* Charlottetown, P.E.I.: Gynergy, 1988.

———. *Two Women in a Birth.* Toronto: Guernica, 1994.

Marlatt, Daphne and Nicole Brossard. *Mauve.* Montréal: editions *nbj* no. 40, 1985.

———. *Character / Jeu de letters.* Montréal: editions *nbj* no. 69, 1986.

Marlatt, Daphne and Robert Minden. *Steveston.* Vancouver: Talonbooks, 1974.

———. *Steveston.* 2nd edition. Edmonton, Longspoon, 1984.

———. *Steveston.* 3rd edition. Vancouver: Ronsdale, 2001.

Marlatt, Daphne and Carol Itter, eds. *Opening Doors: Vancouver's East End.* Victoria: Aural History, Provincial Archives of British Columbia, 1979.

Marquez, Gabriel García. *One Hundred Years of Solitude.* New York: Avon, 1970.

Mathur, Ashok, ed. "Race Poetry: an eh-ditorial." Mathur, ed.
　　Prairie Fire 5–10.

———. "Race Poetry, Eh?" *A Poetic Supplement to Prairie Fire*
　　(produced to commemorate UNESCO's world poetry day and the
　　United Nations International Day for the Elimination of Racial
　　Discrimination, March 21, 2001). *Prairie Fire* 21.4 (Winter
　　2000–01).

Marx, Karl. *The Eighteenth Brumaire of Louis Bonaparte*. New
　　York: International, 1963.

McCance, Dawne. "Crossings: An Interview with Erin Mouré."
　　Mosaic 36 (2003): 1–16.

McGann, Jerome, ed. "Postmodern Poetries: Jerome J. McGann Guest-
　　Edits an Anthology of Language Poets From North America and
　　the United Kingdom." *Verse* 7.1 (Spring, 1990): 6–73.

McGonegal, Julie. "Hyphenating the Hybrid 'I': (Re)Visions of
　　Racial Mixedness in Fred Wah's *Diamond Grill*." *Essays on
　　Canadian Writing* 70 (2002): 177–95.

Messerli, Douglas, ed. *The Gertrude Stein Awards in Innovative
　　American Poetry*. Los Angeles: Sun and Moon, 1995.

Morrell, Carol, ed. *Grammar of Dissent: Poetry and Prose by
　　Dionne Brand, Claire Harris, Marlene Nourbese Philip*.
　　Fredericton: Goose Lane, 1994.

Moses, Daniel David and Terry Goldie, eds. *Canadian Literature
　　in English*. Toronto: Oxford UP, 1992.

Moure, Eirin. *Sheep's Vigil by a Fervent Person, A Transelation
　　[sic] of Alberto Caeiro / Fernando Pessoa's O Guardador de
　　Rebanhos*. Toronto: Anansi, 2001.

Mouré, Erin. (See also Eirin Moure.) *A Frame of the Book* (or
　　The Frame of a Book). Toronto: Anansi, 1999.

———. "A Love that Persists." *Books in Canada* 19.9 (December
　　1990): 42–43.

———. *Domestic Fuel*. Toronto: Anansi, 1985.

———. *Empire, York Street*. Toronto: Anansi, 1979.

———. *Furious*. Toronto: Anansi, 1988.

———. *The Green Word: Selected Poems*. Toronto: Oxford UP, 1994.

———. *O Cidadán*. Toronto: Anansi, 2002.

———. *Pillage Laud* (*Moveable Text*). Toronto: Moveable Type
　　Books, 1999.

————. *Search Procedures*. Toronto: Anansi, 1996.

————. *Sheepish Beauty, Civilian Love*. Montréal: Véhicule, 1992.

————. *Visible Spectrum*. Vancouver: pomflit, 1992.

————. *Wanted Alive*. Toronto: Anansi, 1983.

————. *The Whisky Vigil*. Madeira Park, B.C.: Harbour Publishing, 1981.

————. *WSW (West South West)*. Montréal: Véhicule, 1989.

Mouré, Erin and Bronwen Wallace. "Two Women Talking: Correspondence 1985–87." *Quarry* 42.2 (1985–87): 33–50. Rpt. *Two Women Talking: Correspondence 1985–87 Erin Mouré and Bronwen Wallace*. Ed. Susan McMaster. Toronto: Living Archives of The Feminist Caucus of The League of Canadian Poets, 1993.

Naipaul, V.S. *A Way in the World: a novel*. New York: Knopf, 1994.

Nanjo Acosta, Isaías. "Canadian Absences and American Presences in the Poetry of Robert Kroetsch." In Juan Ignacio Oliva et al, eds. *Canadística canaria (1991–2000): ensayos literarios anglocanadienses*. La Laguna: Univ. de La Laguna, 2002. 143–61.

Neuman, Shirley and Robert Wilson. *Labyrinths of Voice: Conversations with Robert Kroetsch*. Edmonton: NeWest Press, 1982.

Neuman, Shirley and Smaro Kamboureli, eds. "A Special Daphne Marlatt Feature." *Line* 13 (1989).

Nichols, Miriam. "Subject of Experience: Post-cognitive subjectivity in the Work of bpNichol and Daphne Marlatt." *Studies in Canadian Literature/Études en literature canadienne* 25.2 (2000): 108–30.

Norris, Ken, ed. *Canadian Poetry Now: 20 Poets of the 80's*. Toronto: General, 1990.

Olson, Charles. *The Maximus Poems*. New York: Jargon/Corinth, 1960.

Ondaatje, Michael, ed. *The Long Poem Anthology*. Toronto: Coach House, 1979.

Perelman, Bob. "The First Person." Perelman, ed. 147–65.

————, ed. "TALKS." *Hills* 6/7 (Spring 1980).

Perloff, Marjorie. *Postmodern Genres*. Norman: U of Oklahoma P, 1989.

Reed, Sabrina. "'Against the Source': Daphne Marlatt's Revision of Charles Olson." *Studies in Canadian Literature* 26.1 (Winter 2001): 132–44.

Rimanelli, Giose, ed. *Modern Canadian Stories*. Toronto: Ryerson Press, 1966.

Rich, Adrienne. *Of Woman Born: motherhood as experience and institution*. New York: Norton, 1976.

Rosenfield, Israel. *The Invention of Memory*. New York: Basic Books, 1988.

Rudy, Susan. "'& how else can i be here?': reading cross-wise through some poetries of Canada." *Huk* 284–98.

———. "'But is it Politics?': Jeff Derksen's 'Rearticulatory Poetics'." In Pauline Butling and Susan Rudy, *Writing in Our Time: Canada's Radical Poetries in English (1957–2003)*. Waterloo: Wilfrid Laurier UP, 2005.

———. "'what can atmosphere with / vocabularies delight?': Excessively Reading Erin Mouré." In Pauline Butling and Susan Rudy, *Writing in Our Time: Canada's Radical Poetries in English (1957–2003)*. Waterloo: Wilfrid Laurier UP, 2005.

Silliman, Ron. "The New Sentence." Perelman, ed. 190–99.

Saul, Joanne. "Displacement and self-representation: theorizing contemporary Canadian biotexts." *Biography: An Interdisciplinary Quarterly* 24:1 (2001): 259–72.

Saunders, Philip and Justin Thompson. "The Missing Women of Vancouver." *CBC News indepth:Pickton*. Updated Jan. 27, 2004. <www.cbc.ca/news/features/bc_missingwomen.html>

Schwartz, Leonard. "International not Ultranational: New writing from the new New York." *Literary Review* 46 (2003): 231–33.

Sellery, J'nan Morse. "Robert Kroetsch and Aritha van Herk on Writing & Reading Gender and Genres: An Interview." *Canadian Literature* 170/171 (2001): 21–55.

Sinclair, Jr., Gordon. *The J.J. Harper Story*. Toronto: McClelland and Stewart, 1999.

Sloan, Mary Margaret, ed. *Moving Borders: Three Decades of Innovative Writing by Women*. New Jersey: Talisman House, 1998.

Snyder, Gary. *Earth House Hold: Technical Notes and Queries to follow Dharma Revolutionaries*. New York: New Directions, 1957.

Souster, Raymond, ed. *New Wave Canada: The New Explosion in Canadian Poetry*. Toronto: Contact, 1966.

Spanos, William V. "Retrieving Bob Kroetsch on the Occasion of His Seventieth Birthday." *boundary* 2 26.2 (1999): 119–32.

Spender, Dale. *Man Made Language*. London: Routledge and
Kegan Paul, 1980.

Sugars, Cynthia. "'The negative capability of camouflage': fleeing
diaspora in Fred Wah's *Diamond Grill*." *Studies in Canadian
Literature* 26:1 (2001): 27–45.

Suknaski, Andrew. *Wood Mountain Poems*. Toronto: Macmillan,
1976.

Sullivan, Rosemary, ed. *The Oxford Book of Stories by Canadian
Women in English*. Don Mills: Oxford UP, 1999.

———. *Poetry by Canadian Women*. Toronto: Oxford UP, 1989.

Thesen, Sharon, ed. *The New Long Poem Anthology*. Toronto:
Coach House, 1991.

———. *The New Long Poem Anthology*. Second Edition. Vancouver;
Talonbooks, 2001.

Wah, Fred. "A Prefatory Note." *Waiting for Saskatchewan*. n.p.

———. *Alley Alley Home Free*. Red Deer: Red Deer College P, 1992.

———. *Among*. Toronto: Coach House, 1972.

———. *Breathin' My Name with a Sigh*. Vancouver: Talonbooks,
1981.

———. *Diamond Grill*. Edmonton: NeWest, 1996.

———. *Earth*. Canton, N.Y.: Institute of Further Studies, 1974.

———. *Faking It: Poetics and Hybridity Critical Writing 1984–
1999*. Edmonton: NeWest, 2000.

———. *Grasp the Sparrow's Tail*. Privately published, Kyoto,
1982. Rpt. in *Waiting for Saskatchewan* 29–56.

———. *Lardeau: Selected First Poems*. Toronto: Island, 1965.

———. *Limestone Lakes Utaniki*. Designed by Peter Bartl. Red
Deer: Red Deer College P & The Press at Crawford Bay, 1989.
Rpt. in Wah, *So Far*: 65–72.

———. *Loki is Buried at Smoky Creek: Selected Poems*. Vancouver:
Talonbooks, 1980.

———. "Lullabye [sic] and Sea." In *By Land and Sea (Prospect
and Refuge)*. Marian Penner Bancroft. Vancouver: Presentation
House Gallery, 2000. n.p.

———. *Mountain*. Buffalo: Audit, 1967.

———. *Music at the Heart of Thinking*. Red Deer: Red Deer
College P, 1987.

———. *Pictograms from the Interior of B.C.* Vancouver: Talonbooks, 1975.

——. "Race, to Go." Mathur, ed., "The Skin on Our Tongues"
1993. Spec. Issue of *Absinthe*. Precedes 6.1 (Summer 1993).
Edited by Ashok Mathur, Suzette Mayr and Hiromi Goto-
Tongu: 36.

——. *So Far*. Vancouver: Talonbooks, 1991.

——. *Tree*. Writing Series. Vol. 9. Vancouver: Vancouver Community Press, 1972.

——. *Waiting for Saskatchewan*. Vancouver: Turnstone Press,
1985.

Wallace, Mark and Steven Marks, eds. *Telling it Slant: Avant-
Garde Poetics of the 1990s*. Tuscaloosa: U of Alabama P, 2002.

Warland, Betsy, ed. *InVersions: writing by dykes, queers &
lesbians*. Vancouver: Press Gang, 1991.

Watten, Barrett. "Russian Formalism & The Present." Perelman,
ed. 50–73.

Wayman, Tom and Calvin Wharton, eds. *East of Main*. Vancouver:
Pulp, 1989.

Wiens, Jason. "'Language seemed to split in two': national
ambivalence (s) and Dionne Brand's 'no language is neutral.'"
Essays on Canadian Writing 70 (Spring 2000): 81–102.

Williams, Eric. *Capitalism and Slavery*. Chapel Hill: U of North
Carolina P, 1944.

Williams, William Carlos. *Paterson*. New York: New Directions, 1963.

Williamson, Janice. "'It gives me a great deal of pleasure to say
yes': Writing/Reading Lesbian in Daphne Marlatt's *Touch to
My Tongue*." Barbour, ed. 171–93.

——, ed. *Sounding Differences: Conversations with Seventeen
Canadian Women Writers*. Toronto: U of Toronto P, 1993.

Winks, Robin W. *The Blacks in Canada, A History*. Montreal:
McGill-Queen's UP, 1971.

The Women & Words Committee, eds. *Women & Words: The
Anthology / les femmes et les mots: une anthologie*. Harbour
Publishing, 1984.

Yougmin, Kim. "The Experimental Spirit in Canadian Poetry:
Margaret Atwood, Eli Mandel, George Bowering and the
Experimental Poets Thereafter." *Journals of English Language
and Literature / Youngo Youngmunhak* 49.4 (2003): 755–80.

Index

Adorno, Theodor, 124
Alexie, Sherman, 95
Allen, Lillian, 71
Allison, Gaye, 75
Althusser, Louis, 131, 135
Andrews, Bruce, 129
Andrews, Craig, 149
Annharte [Marie Annharte
    Baker], 89–113
  biocritical introduction,
    89–92
  on *Being on the Moon*,
    97–100
  on "Coyote Columbus
    Cafe," 101–7
  on *Exercises in Lip
    Pointing*, 107–13
  on gender inequality, 110–
    11
  on her historical contexts,
    93–99, 109–13
  on humour, 94–97, 101–4
  on hybridity, 109–12
  on language and
    colonization, 100–108

on sex trade workers,
    111–12
  Wah on, 159
Annharte [Marie Annharte
    Baker], works
  "Albeit Original" (play), 91
  Being on the Moon, 90–91,
    97–100, 107–8
  "Blueberry Canoe," 92
  "Borrowing Enemy
    Language," 89, 91,
    100–101
  "Cherries Could Be a Girl's
    Best," 92
  Coyote Columbus Cafe, 91,
    101–7, 108, 109
  "Coyote Columbus Cafe,"
    91, 96, 101–7
  "Coyotrix Recollects," 92
  "Dark Love," 100
  "Discovery is a hard act to
    follow," 104–6
  Exercises in Lip Pointing,
    91–92, 107–13
  "Granny Going," 99–100

"How to Stop Writing
About Indians," 112–13
"Hudson's Bay Bill," 98
"I Make Sense of My World
Through Writing," 92
"The Indian Act," 96–97
"I Want to Dance Wild
Indian Black Face,"
109–10
"JJ Bang Bang," 108
"Manifesto for First
People," 94
"Medicine Lines," 92
"Memory Fishes," 91–92
"Moon Bear," 97, 98
"Mr. Indian," 96
"once more it's Indian
time," 101–3
"Raced Out to Write this
Up," 90, 100
"Red Stone Lake," 92
"Squaw Pussy," 92, 110–12
"what does a poor coyote
girl do?", 103–4
Armah, Ayi Kwei, 85
Armour, Richard, 94
Artspeak gallery (Vancouver),
128
Asad, Talal, 139
Ashbery, John, 7–8
Atwood, Margaret, 49

Bahktin, Mikhaïl, 124, 132–33
Baker, Marie Annharte.
See Annharte [Marie
Annharte Baker]
Bambara, Toni Cade, 85
Bancroft, Marian Penner, 145,
169

Banff Centre, 128
Baraka, Amiri [LeRoi Jones],
69, 70, 78
Barthes, Roland, 5–6
Bartl, Peter, 169
Bataille, Georges, 124
Beckman, Lanny, 167
Bernstein, Charles, 129
bilingualism and biculturalism,
146, 163–65
Birney, Earle, 120, 121
Bitter, Sabine, 115
Black, Ayanna, 71, 75
Black Education Project
(Toronto)
Brand on, 69, 71, 78
Black Students' Union,
University of Toronto, 69
Blaise, Clark, 122
Bök, Christian, 135
Borges, Jorge Luis, 6
boundary 2
"A Canadian Issue," 1, 5
founding by Kroetsch and
Spanos, 1, 6, 7
Bowering, George, 22, 49, 120,
149–50
works: *Kerrisdale Elegies*, 40
bpNichol. *See* Nichol, bp
Braithwaite, Kamau, 68,
79–80, 85
Brand, Dionne, 63–87
biocritical introduction,
63–66
on feminism, 75–77, 82–85
on *Fireweed*, 75
on her films, 86–87
on her historical contexts,
67–82

on lesbian experience and
    writing, 77, 78, 80–81
on oral histories, 85–87
on *Spear*, 70–71, 78
on use of the demotic,
    71–74
on women's experience and
    writing, 77, 82–85
Wah on, 167
Brand, Dionne, works
In Another Place, Not Here,
    65, 74
"Anti-Poetry," 79
"Blossom," 72–73
Bread Out of Stone, 64
*Chronicles of the Hostile
    Sun*, 64, 79, 81
"Defense of Claudia," 64
Earth Magic, 64
films, 66, 86–87
'*Fore Day Morning*, 64
*At the Full & Change of
    the Moon*, 65–66
Land to Light On, 63, 65
*A Map to the Door of No
    Return*, 64
No Burden to Carry, 64
No Language Is Neutral,
    64–65, 72–74, 80–81, 84
"no language is neutral," 73
Primitive Offensive, 64, 79
Rivers Have Sources, 64, 82
Sans Souci, 65
thirsty, 63, 65
"this is you girl," 80–81
*We're Rooted Here and
    They Can't Pull Us Up*,
    87
Winter Epigrams, 64, 79

Brathwaite, J. Ashton
    [Odimumba Kwamdela],
    70
Bristow, Peggy, 87
Brooks, Gwendolyn, 77, 82
Brossard, Nicole
    Marlatt on, 31, 36, 38
    Wah on, 38
    works: *character/jeu de
        letters*, 25; *Daydream
        Mechanics*, 38; *Mauve*,
        25
Browne, Colin, 122, 123, 125,
    129
Butling, Pauline
    as DTUC instructor, 121–22
    Wah and, 145, 167

Cabri, Louis, 132, 135, 168
Canadian Indian Youth
    Council, 95
Carr, Brenda, 36
Carter, Martin, 68, 85
Carty, Linda, 87
Case, Fred, 78
Castro, Fidel, 77
Césaire, Aimé, 85
Child, Abigail, 129
Choy, Wayson, 167
Cliff, Michelle, 81
Clifford, James, 139
Contemporary Art Gallery
    (Vancouver), 128
Contemporary Verse 2, 97
Contrast, 70
Cooley, Dennis, 16–17
Cooper, Afua, 87
Corman, Cid, 33
Creeley, Robert, 9, 33

Davey, Frank, 144

David Thompson University Centre (DTUC), 120–23, 144

Davies, Kevin, 125, 138

de Beauvoir, Simone, 41, 82

de Beck, Brian, 167

Derksen, Jeff, 115–42
  biocritical introduction, 115–17
  on cultural and urban poetics, 123–31, 134–37, 140–42
  on DTUC, 120–23
  on _Dwell_, 137–40
  on gender issues, 137
  on global capitalism, 131–32, 135–37
  on his historical contexts, 119–31
  on KSW, 122–25, 128–29, 135, 141
  on Language poets, 124–25, 127, 132–33, 135, 140, 141
  on social class, 135–36, 140–41
  on the academy, 133–34
  on web publishing, 132
  on _Writing_, 128–29
  Wah on, 160
  website, 117

Derksen, Jeff, works
  But Could I Make a Living from It, 116
  Down Time, 116, 125, 132, 140–41
  Dwell, 116, 134, 137–40
  "Excursives," 139–40

"Fixed City & Mobile World," 116

"Hold On To Your Bag Betty," 139–40

"Jerk," 131–32

"Jobber," 132

Memory Is the Only Thing Holding Me Back, 116

"Neighbourhood," 137–40

Selfish, 116

Transnational Muscle Cars, 115, 116–17, 135

Until, 116

"Until," 132

Dickinson, Peter, 90–91

Douglas, Frederick, 77

Douglas, Stan, 128

DTUC. _See_ David Thompson University Centre (DTUC)

DuBois, W.E.B., 77

Duff, Wilson, 95

Duncan, Robert, 40

Ear Inn, Segue reading series, 129, 135

Edelman, Gerald, 52, 60

Emmett, Kirsten, 48

Fanon, Franz, 77

Fawcett, Brian, 141–42

Ferguson, Deanna, 121, 125, 141

Firestone, Shulamith, 82

Fireweed, 75

Fitzgerald, Judith, 65

Foran, Charles, 165

Fry, Hedy, 164–65

Gates, Henry Louis, 72
Georgia Straight (Vancouver), 70
Gilbert, Gerry, 120, 121
Ginsberg, Alan, 142
Giovanni, Nikki, 70, 77, 82
Goldman, Emma, 82
Gom, Leona, 120, 121
Gossett, Hattie, 111
Gramsci, Antonio, 132, 141
Grenier, Robert, 140
Grinning Rectos of Late Capitalism (Vancouver), 125
Grossberg, Lawrence, 131
Guevera, Che, 77
Gunnars, Kristjana, 97

Hall, Phil, 48
Hamilton, Sylvia, 87
Harper, J.J., 108–9
Harris, Claire, 72
Hauser, Gwen, 75
Hejinian, Lyn, 127, 129
Hindmarch, Gladys, 167
Howe, Susan, 14, 129
Hryniuk, Angela, 121
Hudson, Noel, 121

Immigrant Women's Centre (Toronto), 78, 82
Ismail, Jam, 159

Jaeger, Peter, 135
Jakobson, Roman, 138
Jam, The (punk band), 135
James, C.L.R., 67, 69
Jarraway, David, 45
Johnson, Charles, 85
Jones, Gayle, 85

Jones, LeRoi. *See* Baraka, Amiri [LeRoi Jones]
Joseph, Clifton, 71

Kamboureli, Smaro, 20, 164
Kareda, Urjo, 78
Kinesis (Vancouver), 48
Kogawa, Joy, 149
Kootenay School of Writing (KSW)
    Derksen on, 122–25, 128–29, 135, 141
Kroetsch, Robert, 1–22
    biocritical introduction, 1–3
    boundary 2 founding and role, 1, 6, 7
    on concealment of self, 13
    on cosmology and excess, 18–19
    on ethics, 21–22
    on gender and writing, 18–21
    on his agency, 11–13
    on his early life, 8–9, 12, 18, 20
    on his historical contexts, 5–9, 22
    on his use of couplets, 15–16
    on parody, 20–22
    on place, 8–9, 12
    on "Poem for my Dead Sister," 14–17
    on postmodernism, 5–7, 21–22
    on resistance and affirmation, 17–18
    on sound, 16–17
    on subliterary texts, 12–13, 18

on systems and structure,
13–14, 21
on the line and line-
endings, 9–11
Kroetsch, Robert, works
Completed Field Notes, 2,
16–17, 20
"The Criminal Intensities
of Love as Paradise," 16
*Excerpts from the Real
World*, 13
Field Notes, 2, 8
"For Play and Entrance," 21
The Hornbooks of Rita K, 2
"I Wanted to Write a
Manifesto," 12
The Ledger, 12–13
A Likely Story, 12, 14–17
"Poem for My Dead
Sister," 14–17
"The Poetics of Rita
Kleinhart," 2
"The Poet's Mother," 17, 20
The Puppeteer, 20
*Revisions of Letters
Already Sent*, 10–11, 13
The Sad Phoenician, 18
Seed Catalogue, 12
The Snowbird Poems, 2–3
The Stone Hammer Poems, 2
KSW. *See* Kootenay School of
Writing (KSW)

Laclau, Ernesto, 131
Lamming, George, 68, 85
Landale, Zoë, 48
Language poets
Derksen on, 124–25, 127,
132–33, 135, 140, 141

Laser, Hank, 168
Lau, Evelyn, 159
Leacock, Stephen, 94
Lee, Dennis, 163–64
Leome, Don, 70
Levine, Philip, 49
Levy, Andy, 129
Livesay, Dorothy, 49
Liyong, Taban Lo, 85
Lorca, Federico Garcia, 53, 54
Lusk, Dorothy Trujillo, 132,
141

Majzels, Robert, 45
Manerry, Rob, 135
Marlatt, Daphne, 23–41
biocritical introduction,
23–27
Mouré on, 49
on binary oppositions,
36–37, 39
on female experience, 25,
30–32, 37–39
on lesbian concerns, 25, 30,
32, 38–39
on male experience, 31, 37
on memory, 40–41
on phenomenology and
proprioception, 36–37
on prose/poetry genre
blurring, 32–36
on *Salvage*, 29–36, 40–41
on spirituality, 39–40
on the body, 37–39
periodics role, 24–25
Rudy on positionings in, 11
Tessera role, 25
TISH role, 23
Wah on, 148–50, 158

Women & Words
    conference role, 25
Marlatt, Daphne, works
    "A Lost Book," 25–26
    Ana Historic, 25
    "At Birch Bay," 35
    "Booking Passage," 32–34
    "Changing the Focus,"
        40–41
    character/jeu de letters, 25
    Double Negative, 25
    Frames of a Story, 24
    Ghost Works, 25
    "Here and There," 26
    here & there, 26
    How Hug a Stone, 25
    "Impossible Portraiture,"
        26
    leaf leaf/s, 24
    Mauve, 25
    "Musing with
        Mothertongue," 25
    Net Work, 25
    Opening Doors, 24
    *Readings from the
        Labyrinth*, 25
    Rings, 24
    Salvage, 25–26, 29–36,
        40–41
    Steveston, 8, 24, 29, 33–34
    Steveston Recollected, 24
    Taken, 25
    This Tremor Love Is, 25–26
    Touch to My Tongue, 25
    "Tracing the Cut," 26
    Two Women in a Birth, 25
    Vancouver Poems, 24
    What Matters, 24
    Zócalo, 24

Marquez, Gabriel García, 80
Marquis, Don, 94–95
Marx, Karl, and Marxism
    Annharte on, 94
    Brand on, 77, 81
    Derksen on, 126, 134, 136,
        138
Mathur, Ashok, 165
Maud, Ralph, 127
McCaffery, Steve, 139–40
McFadden, David, 120
McTair, Roger, 71
Merwin, W.S., 49
Miki, Roy, 149, 157, 163, 164
Misgeld, Dieter, 81
Mitzleholtzu, Edgar, 85
Mouffe, Chantal, 131
Mouré, Erin [Eirin, Erín],
        43–61
    biocritical introduction,
        43–46
    on colloquial language, 58
    on community and
        responsibility, 50, 54
    on female experience and
        writing, 50–51, 53, 55
    on French and English
        languages, 45, 48
    on *Furious*, 47–51
    on her first name, 44, 45
    on identity, 43–44, 47,
        50–51
    on perception, 51–52,
        55–57, 58–61
    on philosophy, 49–50, 58
    on prose poems, 57
    on reading strategies,
        54–57
    on religion, 58

on *Sheepish Beauty*, 52–61
on Women & Words
    conference, 48
translations of others'
    works, 45
Mouré, Erin [Eirin, Erín],
    works
    "The Acts," 51, 53
    "The Curious," 54
    Domestic Fuel, 47
    Empire, York Street, 43–44
    "Everything," 54
    "Executive Suite," 54
    "Fit," 58–59
    A Frame of the Book, 44, 45
    Furious, 44, 47–51, 53
    The Green Word, 44
    "Hope Stories," 57
    Installations, 45
    *Museum of Bone and
        Water*, 45
    "The Notification of
        Birches," 58
    O Cidadán, 43, 45
    Pillage Laud, 43, 44–45
    "Rolling Motion," 44
    Search Procedures, 44, 45, 51
    *Sheepish Beauty, Civilian
        Love*, 44, 50, 52–61
    Sheep's Vigil, 45
    "These Synapses," 58–60
    "Three Versions," 51
    "Visible Spectrum," 53
    "The Vowel O," 54
    The Whisky Vigil, 44
    WSW (*West South West*),
        44, 54
multiculturalism, 149, 163–65

Naipaul, V.S., 67, 68
National Film Board, Studio
    D, 86
National Indian Youth
    Council (U.S.), 95
Native Alliance for Red Power
    (Vancouver), 96
Newlove, John, 122
New Poetics Colloquium
    (Vancouver), 125, 129
Nichol, bp, 7, 98, 147, 158
Nichols, Miriam, 158
Nielson, Melanie, 129
Nkrumah, Kwame, 69

O'Brien, Erin, 120, 139
Odimumba Kwamdela [J.
    Ashton Brathwaite], 70
O'Hara, Frank, 49
Okano, Haruko, 144, 168–69
Olson, Charles
    Derksen on, 120–21, 134
    Kroetsch on, 7–8, 9
    Marlatt on, 35
    Mouré on, 60
    Wah on, 165–66
    works: *The Maximus
        Poems*, 8, 9, 134
Olson, Tillie, 120
Opening Doors, 148
Open Letter, 144, 145
Or Gallery (Vancouver), 128

Padmore, George, 69
Penner, Susan, 49
Perelman, Bob, 124
periodics, 24–25, 150
Perloff, Marjorie, 32
Persky, Stan, 167

Philip, Marlene Nourbese, 71
Pickton, Robert, 111
Piercy, Marge, 49
Poetry Conference and Festival
  (2003), University of
  Calgary, 145
Port Coquitlam serial killer,
  111
Prairie Fire, "Race Poetry, eh?"
  issue, 164–65
Pratt, Mary Louise, 139

Randall, Margaret, 81
Reaney, James, 164
Rich, Adrienne, 49, 64, 82
Romain, Jacques, 85
Rosenfield, Israel, 52
Royal Commission on Bilingu-
  alism and Biculturalism,
  149, 163–64

Sanchez, Sonia, 70, 77, 82, 85
Scheier, Libby, 75
Scott, Gail, 31, 44, 48, 50–51
Scree, 144
Segue reading series (Ear Inn),
  129, 135
Service, Robert, 12, 17
Shadd, Adrienne, 87
Shaw, Nancy, 125, 128
Sheard, Sarah, 75
Sherry, James, 168
Silliman, Ron, 140, 142, 168
Silvera, Makeda, 70, 76
Smith, Dorothy, 81
Snyder, Gary, 166
Sound Heritage, 149
Spanos, William, 1, 6–7, 9
Spear, 70–71, 78

Spender, Dale, 48
Spicer, Jack, 7, 49
Split Shift: A Colloquium on
  the New Work Writing
  (Vancouver), 125, 127
Stanley, George, 123
Stein, Gertrude, 14, 120
Stevens, Wallace, 7, 8
Strudensky, Andrea, 163
Suknaski, Andrew, 148
Swift Current, 144

Tallman, Warren, 7
*Telling It: Women and Lang-
  uage Across Cultures,*
  25
Tessera, 25, 48
The Jam (punk band), 135
Thomas, Audrey, 122
TISH: A POETRY NEWSLETTER,
  23, 121, 143
TISH writers
  Derksen on, 141–42
  Kroetsch on, 7
  Marlatt on, 30–31
  Wah on, 167
Tortino, Mina, 128
Tosh, Bev, 144, 168
Truck Gallery (Calgary), 130
Tuumba Press, 127

Vancouver Industrial Writers
  Union, 43, 48
Vanguard (Vancouver), 127
van Herk, Aritha, 150
Virgo, Sean, 122
Vultures (Vancouver), 125
Vuong-Riddick, Thuong, 165

Wah, Fred, 143–69
  biocritical introduction,
    143–45
  and Butling, 145, 167
  Derksen on, 120–22
  interview with Marlatt,
    37–40
  Kroetsch on, 11, 16, 22
  on *Diamond Grill*, 147–51,
    156–58
  on ethics and social change,
    165–68
  on gender issues, 37–39,
    151, 156–58
  on haibun, haiku, and
    utaniki, 150, 151–55
  on his performance
    projects, 168–69
  on identity and race, 147–
    57, 159–63, 168–69
  on multiculturalism, 163–
    65
  on music and writing, 158
  on oral history, 148–49
  on phenomenological
    poetry, 158–59
  on "Race, to Go," 160–63
  on social class, 155–56, 167
  on spirituality, 39–40
  on *Waiting for Sask-
    atchewan*, 150–55
  Poetry Conference and
    Festival (2003), 145
Wah, Fred, works
  Alley Alley Home Free,
    144
  articulations, 144, 168
  *Breathin' My Name with
    a Sigh*, 144, 147, 151

Diamond Grill, 37–38, 144,
  147–51, 156–58
Earth, 165–66
Faking It, 144, 158–59
"Faking It," 158–59
"Father/Mother Haibun
  #7," 151–52
"Father/Mother Haibun
  #9," 153–54
Grasp the Sparrow's Tail,
  150, 153
High Tea, 169
Lardeau, 8, 144
Limestone Lakes Utaniki,
  169
*Loki Is Buried at Smoky
  Creek*, 144
"Lullabye [xi] and Sea,"
  144–45
Mountain, 8, 144
*Music at the Heart of
  Thinking*, 144, 150, 160
*Pictograms from the
  Interior of B.C.*, 121,
  144, 148
"Race, to Go," 160–63
"Speak My Language," 159
"This Dendrite Map:
  Father/Mother
  Haibun," 151–53
Waiting For Saskatchewan,
  144, 147, 150–55
Walcott, Derek, 85
Wallerstein, Immanuel, 130
Warland, Betsy, 25, 32, 40, 75
Wayman, Tom
  Derksen on, 120–21, 122–
    24, 127, 129, 141
  Mouré on, 48

Webb, Phyllis, 49
Welty, Eudora, 95
Wershler-Henry, Darren, 135
Western Front (Vancouver),
    128
Wharton, Calvin, 121
Wheeler, Dennis, 49
Whitehead, Gary, 121
Williams, Eric, 67
Williams, Raymond, 129
Williams, William Carlos, 7, 8
Williamson, Janice, 47
Winks, Robin W., *Blacks in
    Canada*, 86–87
Women & Words conference
    (Vancouver, 1983), 25,
    48, 78–79
Wong, Rita, 159
Wood, Bill, 128
Wright, James, 49
Writers' Union of Canada
    (TWUC), 145
Writing (Vancouver), 128–29

Ziquing, Zhang, 168
Zukofsky, Louis, 33